Your Eastern Star

by Daniel Logan

YOUR EASTERN STAR

Oriental Astrology, Reincarnation and the Future

William Morrow & Company, Inc., New York

Illustrations appear between pages 32 & 33.

This book is dedicated, with deep gratitude, to
Ryuske Tokunaga *(and the entire Tokunaga family, who cared for me while I was in Japan)*—
Bungo Ozawa—
The Kurayoshi family—
Keiko Kama—
and special thanks to Toyo Ito.

CHAPTER 1

On the green, piny, semitropical, mountainous island of Miyajima, in the southern Inland Sea of Japan, I discovered evidence that I had lived before. Until that time, the one aspect of the extensive work I have done in areas of the occult and psychic phenomena in which I did not particularly believe was reincarnation. The experience that occurred on Miyajima has changed my entire life.

I had gone to Japan in the early part of 1970 to collect information for this book, which was to be solely about astrology and psychic awareness as practiced in the Orient. From my earliest memory I have been attracted to Japan and fascinated by things Japanese. It never once crossed my mind, at least on a conscious level, that my near-fanatic infatuation with the country, its people and culture, was owing to a desire to return, spiritually as well as physically, to where I had been before.

Having lived in Japan for two months, I was now about to embark on the one most significant spiritual happening of my life thus far. I was to find out the true meaning of "going home," something I have never been able to do in my own country.

With my friend and interpreter, Ryuske Tokunaga, pronounced *Ru-skay Toe-koo-na-ga* (see Plate 1), I had traveled to several cities and had stayed in the homes of Japanese people—eating, sleeping, and, generally, living as they do. The horrendous, shattering, disheartening vibrations of Hiroshima had been too much for me to bear, and we had left that tragic city of death two days earlier than scheduled, affording us an additional amount of time before traveling to Kyushu, the southernmost of the four major islands that make up Japan.

"We have some extra time, and there are several interesting places close by," Ryuske suggested. "One of them is the Itsukushima Shrine. The largest wood torii gate in Japan is located there."

I went to one of my guidebooks and found that this particular torii gate, facing the entrance of the Itsukushima Shrine, was the one built out on the sea and often photographed because of its tremendous size and impressive beauty (see Plate 2).

I cannot recall when I had first seen a photograph of this torii gate, but for some reason, possibly because of its being in the water, it has intrigued me more than torii gates that front most sacred shrines of the Buddhist religion.

I expressed a desire to visit the Itsukushima Shrine on Miyajima, and the next morning we departed Hiroshima station, arriving at our destination one hour later. We were fortunate, as it was not a weekend, nor a Japanese holiday, which would have meant our having to contend with an overwhelming mass of pilgrims, who visit the shrines and temples annually. We would be able to explore the island at our leisure, without the pressure of crowds, and I could go into meditation, something I had become accustomed to doing at each shrine and temple visited.

The island of Miyajima is nineteen miles in circumference. It is a sacred island to the Japanese people and, for its size, is still relatively uninhabited. In fact, up until the close of World War II, it was so hallowed and venerated that no births or deaths were permitted there. Pregnant women, the very old, and persons who were ill were shipped to the mainland.

The Itsukushima Shrine was built in the thirteenth century. The buildings of the shrine are connected by mazelike, covered corridors, or galleries, which were also erected out over the water on wooden supports. At high tide, the seemingly endless corridors appear to float on the sea. The entire idea fascinated me, and as we left the train and walked the short distance to the ferry that would take us to Miyajima, the joy in my anxiety could not be contained. I am instantly overpowered by beauty, be it natural or manmade, to the point of childishness, and I realized that this was the one major factor of my personality that grated on Ryuske's Oriental calm and control. On this day, I would have to work doubly hard at maintaining my composure.

The landing dock for the ferry was built on a huge wooden raft. It had a pagodalike roof, from the corners of which hung elaborate metal lanterns that had turned a soft green from constant exposure to the ocean water. As the dock gently swayed above the undulating sea beneath it the lanterns were set into motion, causing them to catch and reflect the rays of a brilliant midmorning sun.

The ferry was in itself a work of art. Also pagoda-topped, the boat was further enhanced by an ornate, ten-foot-tall, wood-carved, hand-painted dragon, which protruded from the bow. Its long neck was covered with black and white scales. A massive red, yellow, and black head sprouted fierce-looking horns. A half-open mouth exposed pointed, angular fangs. Vermilion wood flames leaped from out of the corners of the dragon's mouth. Enchanting and frightening at the same time, it reminded me of a typical villainous Disney character.

With a mere handful of passengers aboard, the ship left its mooring place and put out to sea. Through white-capped waves, the dragon's head bobbed, ever so erect and foreboding. At night, or in a fog, those commanding an approaching vessel could very easily, with justification, feel that they had encountered a monster from the depths.

Silver flashes of blinding sunlight were mirrored into our eyes as the eighteen-hundred-foot-high peaks of Miyajima loomed nearer every knot of the way.

Appearing at first as a speck on the horizon, the true massiveness of Itsukushima's famed torii gate became apparent as our boat chugged toward it. The sensations of goose-bumps and a shooting pain in the pit of my stomach became extremely evident. The reason for this physical discomfort was a strongly manifested feeling of *déjà-vu*—the impression of having traveled over that body of water before, of having stood at the bow of a ship that was headed toward that torii gate, with the mountainous island behind, rising sharply out of the blue-green waters. I brushed the feeling off as an effect of my excitement caused by the immense beauty of the scene that lay before my eyes.

We docked on an opposite side of the island, away from the torii gate. The landing area was more than a bit disappointing, as it consisted of many stalls, gift shops, and restaurants, the scourge of all mankind the world over. (I had been truly surprised when our astronauts did not find a Howard Johnson's on the moon.)

Hurriedly, we left the souvenir stands behind and headed directly for the Itsukushima Shrine. I was on to something. I began to withdraw into myself and became quiet, which for me is a feat in itself.

The roadway was made of well-packed, hardened earth, and was ever curving. Rarely does one find a straight road in the Orient. There is a reason for this. It is to remind one that life too is never straight; that in order to reach a destination, whether it be physical or spiritual, one's path is filled with curves and sudden stops. Little, if anything, is created in the Orient without some spiritual ideal behind it.

As we turned one of the myriad bends in the road, I came to an abrupt halt. Directly in front of us, erected over the road, was a gray stone torii gate, flanked on either side by two massive bronze lions. It framed both the Itsukushima Shrine and the seaward torii gate, which stood a few hundred yards beyond. My heart leaped. I had viewed this scene before. Had it been a photograph in a book? A dream? Neither of these; there was a definite memory of having walked the road before, of having come upon the two guardian lions and of having taken in the vista presently in my line of vision (see Plate 5).

Everything seemed familiar to me. The wind-lashed pine trees that bent toward the water. The thick vegetation that stopped only at the sea's edge. The long corridors of the shrine, neatly structured in a protective, perfectly half-moon-shaped inlet. And especially the mammoth torii gate, its shades of pink, black, and vermilion glisteningly reproduced in the quivering sea that surrounded and splashed beneath it.

At the entrance of the corridors, we removed our shoes and were given slippers, to protect the highly polished and cared-for mahogany floors from being damaged. The roofs of the corridors were tightly woven and matted stalks of grass. Like the roofs of Japanese farmhouses, they rarely leak and last for many years. I passed over the shining black floors in a dream-like state of consciousness.

Vermilion-painted camphor-wood posts held the roofs up. There were no walls, only a short, intricately designed guard rail protected one from the sea a few feet below. Occasionally, I would stop and sit on the railing (see Plate 4). At this point, I had almost total recall of having passed through the corridors previously. My being was filled with a kind of peace, a restful tranquillity that I hardly, if ever, had experienced previously or since then.

Constantly in view was the Itsukushima torii gate. From almost any vantage point on the island, whether it was at sea level or high in the mountains, the torii gate was visible. In centuries past, fishermen, sailors, and anyone putting out to sea would navigate their ships between the colossal camphor-wood posts of the gate. This was said to afford the traveler a safe return from his voyage.

Facing one of the corridors, on stilts of its own, about twenty feet away was a small, covered platform. Its wood was ancient and crumbling. As I looked at the platform, I felt that it was a theater of some kind. Ryuske read the inscription. The edifice had indeed once been a theater and had, in recent years, been designated a National Treasure. Hundreds of years ago, neighboring kings and noblemen would come and behold sacred dances and rites that were performed by the priests and monks of Itsukushima. I was effortlessly transported to another time and could envision elaborately costumed performers. They were dressed in hues of reds and oranges. On their heads were large, ornamented headpieces. We were later to learn that the monks of Itsukushima still wear bright yellow, orange, and red costumes with elaborate headgear when celebrating certain religious rites.

"Do you feel ill?" Ryuske inquired, with deep concern about my almost trancelike state.

"I'm fine," I half-consciously responded, realizing an explanation might really permit him to think that something was the matter with me.

"Where do you think the deer are?" I added, not in the least aware of the words I spoke. We had left the corridors and were on the island itself.

"What deer?" Ryuske acknowledged my question with one of his own. "I don't think there are any deer here; this is an island, far from land."

Within moments, a herd of half-tame deer did come down to the edge of the water to forage for food and to drink (see Plate 7).

"How did you know there were deer here?" Ryuske asked. He knew that I was a psychic by profession and was beginning to discern the reason for my apparent feverlike condition.

My love for animals brought me to reality long enough for

us to purchase packets of food from a vendor and to feed these aggressive, butting, somewhat dangerous creatures.

A group of students approached us in their black, brass-buttoned, Nehru-collared uniforms and asked me to pose with them for photographs. In Japan, one must get accustomed to the adulation heaped on foreigners, especially Americans. In the smaller cities and hamlets of Japan, one is followed and photographed by enraptured children. If they discover that you are an American, you are usually asked for an autograph as well. Do not ever believe the stories that Americans are resented and disliked in Japan. These are lies, possibly spread by visiting American businessmen who have met their match in trading with their highly intelligent and aware Japanese counterparts.

I posed with one of the students, and within minutes, what seemed like dozens of children appeared with their cameras. One never forgets the joy and sheer delight of a pack of these students after they have completed their mission of picture taking with you. Their day has been made, and the photographs will be looked at often and cherished forever.

One of the most vivid memories of Japan that will always stay with me occurred when a group of Japanese students in Hiroshima asked me for autographs. Anyone the least bit sensitive cannot but feel the morbid vibrations of Hiroshima. The pain and horror of that fatal day of August 6, 1945, still remain in the atmosphere. To me, it is as though the bomb had been dropped yesterday instead of a quarter of a century ago.

The museum in Hiroshima that houses vivid mementos of the agony inflicted upon the people of this city—photographs, movies, pieces of clothing, items that had melted in the inferno and come together to form new sculpture, waxen replicas of still living, scarred and burned humans—is both shocking and damaging to one's sense of human understanding and credibility.

As we came to the exit of the museum, a group of students surrounded me. At first I was a bit frightened, for had I been in their place, I would have certainly felt the need for retaliation of some kind, or at least I would have demanded an explanation (see Plate 6). So, I was a bit astonished by their warmth and friendliness.

"Don't they know that I am an American?" I wondered. "Don't they know that Americans perpetrated this tragedy upon their elders?"

Their reply was simple and direct—they realized the bomb had been dropped by Americans, but there had been a war and, in the Japanese tradition, whoever won a war was to be respected. They also realized that America had helped to rebuild their war-torn land and had been instrumental in bringing about their present prosperity.

The understanding and adaptability of the Oriental mind, even in their young children, is beyond Western man's thinking.

In Osaka, at the beginning of my stay in Japan, Ryuske's uncle had asked me to pose with him in his home. What he said, translated by Ryuske, will not ever be forgotten. "Tell Daniel-san, now that I have had an American in my home, and I have taken photographs with him, I can die with happy memories. My life is complete." His eyes shone with tears, and I knew that this was not merely an example of Japanese politeness—he truly meant it. In World War II he had lost not only friends but a few relatives as well. Would I ever learn to be as forgiving, kindly, and loving as the Japanese people?

After I had posed with the students, Ryuske suggested that we hike up into the hills. We did so, pausing now and then to look down onto the thatched roofs of Itsukushima Shrine, and the ever-present, haunting torii gate.

The hills were dotted with houses made of pine, covered by black-tiled roofs. Every so often, a person would stop his daily activity and greet us with a splendid grin. Children would stop their playing and carefully, smilingly observe us.

We chanced upon a five-storied, brilliant-orange pagoda. Besides its apparent beauty, this particular pagoda was noted for its tremendous strength, having withstood countless severe typhoons and earthquakes. A Japanese tourist visiting the pagoda enlightened us. He said it was still in exactly the same condition as it was the day it was created. This is quite rare for five-storied, fragile pagodas in Japan. Many such pagodas have been completely restored, every section of them having been replaced at one time or another (see Plate 3).

I was once again struck with the feeling that I had traversed this terrain before. I have few dreams that I can remember; however, there is a recurring one that takes place in an area exactly like that surrounding the magnificent orange pagoda. Dark-green moss covers the earth in this dream, and I can sense a dampness. White stones are placed here and there, forming no special pattern, kept as natural as possible. Pine trees, shrubs, and tall grass grow on sloping hills behind the pagoda. My dream had become a reality. I would have been perfectly able to describe this section of Miyajima before I saw it in actuality.

Ryuske started back toward the main road, but I stopped him. "There's something more I want to see. Let's go around to the back of the pagoda," I said.

"How do you know there is something else here?" Ryuske asked.

"I don't know, I just feel there is."

Behind the pagoda, slightly off to the right, was a decaying, abandoned, large wooden temple. Paint had peeled from the wood, leaving exposed planks of dark browns and grays. Between many of the planks grew moss or fungus.

Ryuske approached someone who appeared to be a resident of the island, rather than a tourist, in hopes that a substantial history of the temple might be forthcoming. The reply was that a very wealthy merchant from the mainland had built the temple many years ago, long before this century.

I walked around the temple three times, not realizing that this was a form of penance at some temples on Miyajima. I could see that Ryuske was becoming perturbed by my actions, or possibly frightened.

We took another path and climbed up over the rocky hills. I began to experience chills, and my brow was wet with perspiration. I was now walking ahead of Ryuske, leading the way in a land where I had not been before in this lifetime.

In a thickly overgrown garden, set off the road, with a tall gate and fence surrounding it, stood a small, very attractive, seemingly comfortable house. Clusters of tall bamboo sheltered it from the hot afternoon sun (see Plate 8).

I went to the gate and tried to open it. Ryuske reprimanded me. In my anxiety, I was losing all my manners. Ryuske asked me why I had tried the gate.

"I wanted to go into the garden, to see the house at closer range. Ryuske, I know you don't believe me, but I have really been here before, in another lifetime. I can remember going into that house. It is some kind of temple, and I can recall praying there."

He looked at me askance and then called over to a maid who had emerged from the house. They chatted for a while. How I wished I knew more of the Japanese language at that moment. Ryuske returned and the maid reentered the house. For a moment he didn't speak and simply walked on.

He finally turned to me and said, "It is not a temple. That house is the private home of a writer."

I didn't know whether to be relieved or disappointed. With no outward sign of emotion, typically Japanese, Ryuske added, "However, many, many years ago, it was a temple of sorts!"

My God, it was true! I had just begun to intellectualize the entire experience. I must have read about Miyajima in a book or magazine. Maybe I had seen pictures in some edition of *National Geographic* and forgotten it. But this current bit of evidence could not be explained so logically. The house had no signs of being a temple, presently or in the past. And it was rather small to be a temple in the first place.

I could feel the blood quicken in my veins. I was in the midst of a reincarnation phenomenon.

"Oh, they'll never believe this one back home!" I said, in a tone mocking the renowned explanation of tourists since time immemorial. I had enough wits about me to take photographs of everything I saw, even individual trees, plants, and stones along the way. I had to know I was not dreaming. To this very day, I am positive that Ryuske thought I had become unglued, or, as the Japanese people say, *Kru-Kru-Pa!*

I raced ahead once more. To my mind there came a flash, a stone wall made of large round boulders, piled on top of one another, retaining a precarious hill from collapsing onto a few houses that stood at the foot of it.

I turned a corner on the path, and there was the wall (see Plate 10), exactly as I had envisioned it a moment before. The only marked difference was that several layers of concrete blocks had been placed on top of the boulders in recent years.

By this time, Ryuske had decided that he had had enough of my raving mind and rushing body and said that we should go back down, as the later it got, the fewer the ferry boats.

"Let us go just a bit farther. I want to see the stone steps."

"What stone steps?" he asked.

Before he had the question out, we rounded a bend, and to the left of us, overgrown and unused for what may have been ages, were a series of about twenty pieces of carved stones, placed in a stairlike manner up a particularly steep hill (see Plate 9). I gave a sharp cry of recognition and raced up the stone steps. I knew there was a small shrine at the top of the stairs. I knew it was there, for I could now remember climbing the stairs so often before. I reached the summit and found the remains of a foundation, not more than thirty feet square. I could sense the building that once stood on the foundation. It resembled the brilliant-orange pagoda, only not as large.

I could faintly hear Ryuske's voice, somewhere in the distance, calling to me, but my mind was in another time. I saw myself in white, flowing robes, the garment of a novice Buddhist priest. My head was shaven. I assumed the lotus position for meditation in the center of the thickly overgrown foundation and prayed.

I had returned to where I had lived, walked and meditated before, not in this present body, not in this current life. No one can tell me differently. No longer would I be able to question reincarnation. How could I, with the otherwise unexplainable proof that had been afforded me.

After meditation, I knew that my confrontation with a past life was coming to an end. There were no more reasons to remain on Miyajima. I had found what only my subconscious had known it was looking for. I went back down the stairs.

Ryuske Tokunaga and I ambled back to the dragon ferry, which returned us to the mainland. It was almost a week before I could regain my composure, before I could come down from the experience that had made me as high as any drug might have. In reality, I did not wish to come down—after all, I had been away from "home" a long, long time.

CHAPTER II

Before we go further, I think it important to express what I feel reincarnation is, or at least how I found it to be defined in the Orient. The question-and-answer method might be the quickest way to do this.

QUESTION: What is reincarnation?

ANSWER: The extensive Oriental belief in reincarnation is very similar to that practiced by theosophists in the West. And that is, that reincarnation is actually not a succession of different lives but rather one continuing, everlasting existence, the various earthly manifestations in different human bodies being a part of the whole soul experience.

The soul remains the same throughout eternity, belonging

to the higher realms (the spiritual) but must descend to the lower realms (the material) in order for it to further its development and attainment through earthly experiences.

Because one lifetime is generally a mere seventy or eighty years, the soul must return many times; one life manifestation on earth is not enough for the soul to progress. Every soul eventually attains enlightenment and goes on to remain in the higher realms when the earthly experiences are no longer needed. With some, it takes longer than others.

Each of us has come across highly advanced and developed souls in our present life. Unfortunately, we have also known many souls that have not progressed. These souls must return and, through the process of Karma, will have opportunities to advance.

QUESTION: What is Karma?

ANSWER: Karma is an Indian word that means "action." In the Eastern teachings of reincarnation, it means the actions of the soul that either propel it forward or hold it back from spiritual progression. When a man is born, and subsequently reborn, on earth, he carries with him the "Karmic debts" of past lives. If he has in any way harmed the natural evolvement of any soul (his own included), then his soul comes back to the earth, reborn in a different body, confronting those souls he has done harm to previously. He then has the opportunity to pay his Karmic debts. "Cause and effect" is another translation of the word *Karma*.

QUESTION: Does one ever come back as an animal or an inanimate object?

ANSWER: Never, as there is nothing one could learn coming back in any form except a human body. Humans alone possess a subconscious mind, the soul.

QUESTION: Why doesn't one recall his past lives?

ANSWER: Everyone has glimpses at one time or another of his past lives. Mostly, they are not recognized as such and are shrugged off as some coincidence or chance occurrence. To know of past lives completely usually is the ability of those persons who have paid most of their Karmic debts and are being made ready for attainment on the next level, their earthly return no longer needed. For the majority of souls, it is difficult enough to contend with the present life, let alone the knowledge of their past existences.

The dramatic experiences on Miyajima were but the climactic events in a lifetime of occurrences involving Japan that can only be interpreted as support for a reincarnation phenomenon. I have tried to intellectualize the following episodes in my life, tried to pass them off as coincidental, tried to place them in some nonpsychic category. But when objectively viewed and recounted, these numerous events can be classified only mystically, psychically.

I was a child when World War II broke out. The children of the small New York City suburb of Whitestone where I grew up would gather together and start playing either cowboy-and-Indian or soldier games. If it was the latter, I always volunteered to portray the Japanese soldier. This was by no means a political preference on my part. I was far too young even to begin to comprehend the intricacies of politics. Rather, I simply desired to be the Japanese.

It seemed more comfortable for me to scream *"Banzai!"* machine-gun the "Americans," and commit hara-kiri with a makeshift wooden sword than it was to be an American infantryman wiping out an enemy battalion with a flamethrower that had been fashioned from a wild-cherry-tree branch.

The movies of the nineteen-forties, picturing all Japanese soldiers as ruthless, sadistic, "buck-toothed, four-eyed, yellow-bellied Nips," were questioned by me even as a youth. I could not believe that every Japanese was a murderous, evil monster, or that each American soldier was strong, tall, good-guy John Wayne. Many of my friends did believe this propaganda. (I assume that adults believed it, too, or there would have been no reason for the notorious "concentration camps" of California in which over one hundred thousand Japanese-American citizens were placed for the duration of the war.)

To this day, there are those amongst my family and friends who feel that my attraction toward Japan was, and is, unpatriotic. When I recently expressed interest in the possibility of marrying a Japanese, one rather bleak aunt hollered bloody murder and said that I should be disowned if I did. When it comes down to fundamentals, we humans have not progressed very far in understanding.

By the time I was ten years old, I had collected two scrapbooks full of photographs of Japan torn from the pages of travel magazines and newspapers. When leafing through the books, I'd be filled with a deep yearning and a feeling of melancholy.

During the war, an importer of Japanese toys and paper goods rented a huge warehouse in our town. He stored everything labeled "Made in Japan" in the cavernous confines of that building. It was against the law to sell anything Japanese in those days, and the importer was waiting out the war so that he could get his goods on the market once again.

My older brother and his friends discovered the building and found a way to get into it. They took many of the five-and-ten-cent-store quality things. Because they felt I was too young to risk being caught, I was not allowed with them on their excursions into the dark, shuttered building. Occasionally, I would be tossed a "treasure"—a paper fan, a tiny umbrella used as a cake decoration, an intricate straw puzzle that joined the two forefingers together so that one was challenged to wrest himself free. How I coveted these items, turning them over and over in my hands. Utilizing an unconscious form of psychometry, I was able to psychically transport myself to the country of their origin.

Born into a strict European-Catholic family, I have always felt something lacking in my religion. Although I consider myself to have been a religious child, I was constantly aware of this feeling of incompleteness.

Down the block from our home stood a house that had a garden containing many trellises covered with climbing roses and ivy. Assisted by a childhood friend, I set up a kind of altar beneath one of the curved, overgrown trellises. Hidden from view, I would bring incense (from the Japanese warehouse) and light it. Contrary to my own religious background, I regarded this place as a temple and not a church. Picking a few choice flowers from my mother's garden, I would stick them into glass jars and place them at the foot of the makeshift shrine.

A discarded chair cover or an old blanket would be fashioned into a robe of sorts. The language used was a pseudo-Oriental jibberish. I have since realized that I was unconsciously attempting to create a Japanese Buddhist ritual—the worship of nature, the lighted incense, the flower offerings.

In grammar school, I won a prize in geography class when I made a pair of Japanese husband-and-wife dolls out of scraps of material, cardboard, and pipe cleaners. The teacher thought the costumes most authentic. I had made them in one afternoon, without a model to copy from. It was one of the few times I was rewarded for my school endeavors.

Like most children, I spent many a rainy afternoon with paper and crayons. I used to create pages of Japanese writing (calligraphy) as I sat on my porch. A cooling summer rain, the smell of newly cut grass, an unmoving, humidity-laden atmosphere, would induce a kind of euphoria from which I could not escape. Hours would pass as I sat on the floor in cross-legged, lotus position, drawing make-believe Japanese letters. I have often wondered whether, if I had kept them, they would have revealed words that have actual meanings.

Japanese motion pictures have always intrigued me. The purposely slow-paced, sometimes actionless, hypnotic films of Japan turn many Westerners away. But I have had an affinity with them since I saw my first one.

In many instances, my personality traits are in direct opposition to my Western background. For example, I have the tendency to read a newspaper or scan a magazine from the back. I work from the last page in. Friends and teachers were always annoyed, not understanding the reasoning behind such an action. It was even discomforting to myself, as I had, naturally, to find the beginning of stories printed on the initial pages of periodicals. It was quite natural for me to pick up a Japanese magazine, where page one is to the left of the binding instead of to the right, and leaf through it from its beginning. (Japanese reads from right to left, unlike English, which reads from left to right.)

As far back as I can remember, I have liked to sleep on the floor. The harder the surface, the better I slept. When I arrived in Japan, it was most easy for me to adapt to sleeping tatami-style—mattresses placed on woven grass mats, directly on the floor.

A few years preceding my visit to Japan, I decided that I must move out of decaying—physically and spiritually—New York City, where I had made my home for years. I investigated the entire northeastern coast, and one area after another was discarded until finally, I came upon some property at the foot of the Catskill Mountain region of New York State. Within an hour after seeing it, I purchased the land. Never having owned property before, I have wondered what made me invest so quickly. The fundamental motivation was that I felt completely at home with the surrounding rolling hills, the sparkling clear streams and lakes, the pointed mountain peaks in the distance, and the deep, green valleys dotted with pine.

One of my Japanese friends, Eji Serita, the artist who did the drawings for the astrology section of this book, visited my country home soon after I acquired it. Both he and his wife became unnaturally silent as I drove them around on a sight-seeing tour.

"What's the matter?" I inquired, afraid they were bored with what I felt to be the nearest thing to heaven.

"No, it is all right," Mrs. Serita assured me. "It is just that . . . well, this place could be the part of Japan where we come from. It is exactly the same as Hokkaido, the most northern island of our country, where we were born, and I guess we are both a little homesick. The only difference is the style of houses, otherwise it is Hokkaido!"

Subconsciously, I had chosen land that was a replica of Japanese terrain.

Buddha had been represented in my home before I even knew who the great Master was. When I was twelve, I found a small stone-carved Buddha on a beach I frequented, which I proceeded to wear around my neck. Whenever I was in the presence of my family, I would discreetly tuck the stone Buddha beneath my undershirt. Otherwise, He would be displayed as vigorously and as prominently as the gold crucifixes and the silver mezuzahs that dangled from the necks of my youthful companions. At the time, I had no conception of Buddha, but I felt a kind of protection whenever I wore His image.

Throughout my life, I have had a recurring dream involving Japanese people, dressed in bright kimonos, scurrying over arched wooden bridges, the clacking of their footwear (*geta*) resounding as clearly as when I was confronted with the actual sound in the ancient city of Kyoto. I recall having this dream even before I went to school.

Ironically, I did not see a Japanese until I was at least seventeen. The first time I conversed with one was after my twentieth birthday.

During the several years I spent as a performer and writer in the elusive art called show business, the best thing I ever wrote was a parody for an off-Broadway revue. The skit was called *Teahouse of the Sympathetic Moon*—a blistering satire combining elements of the two big hits of the era, *Tea and Sympathy* and *Teahouse of the August Moon*. In it I played the leading role. In conception and style, the bit was entirely Japanese, even utilizing Kabuki techniques. I had more compliments on this piece of work than on anything else I ever did, although I wrote it in a short forty-five minutes.

I left my budding (or was it wilting?) theatrical career to become a professional psychic, utilizing an ability I had since childhood. I have told of my experiences in my autobiography, *The Reluctant Prophet* (Doubleday).

There was never any doubt in my mind that I would someday go to Japan. When my friends became successful, they would vacation in France, England, Spain, or Greece. I had only one desire, and that was to see Japan.

My reputation as a psychic burgeoned, and I knew that the time was drawing near when I would at last be able to fulfill my dreams.

I had made countless friends in my new career, and when I expressed interest in a visit to Japan, they would try to dissuade me, saying that I must go instead to India, the cradle of mysticism, the country where psychic awareness began. Somehow, India has never held any interest for me. The spiritual attainment of India is negated by the gross, unspiritual aspects of that country. Though Buddha, the Divine Master of the East, was born in India, there are fewer Buddhists in India today than in any other Oriental country. They have turned from His teachings. How can one have respect for a country where children starve while countless numbers of cows roam the streets, having been pawned off as sacred? The cruelest caste system in history still prevails in India, causing misery and death. Witness Pakistan. I would not exactly call this spiritual evolvement.

In the spring of 1970, the opportunity arose to research material in Japan for this book. I had been introduced to Oriental astrology by my Japanese friends in America, and with the little bits of information offered me by them, I became intrigued and fascinated because of its startling accuracy. What was even more interesting to me was that Oriental astrology is connected to the theory of reincarnation. There was nothing to be found in Western writings about Oriental astrology, and a visit to Japan to gather material on the subject, along with what I could find in respect to reincarnation, seemed like the best approach for this book.

The old adage, "East is east and west is west, and never the twain shall meet," has never applied in my case. Upon my arrival in Japan, I found out why. Immediately, I felt at home in a country that differs so widely from the thoughts, ideals, and actions taught and practiced in the West. In my four-month stay, traveling to more than thirteen cities, I never once felt out of place or "foreign." In fact, I was able to immerse my entire being in Japanese ways of existence. Because of this assimilation and complete understanding of the Japanese spirit, many Japanese called me *hanna gygiin*—the strange foreigner.

Within a short time after my arrival, the distinct sound of the Japanese language, soft and supple yet at the same time strong and determined, fell like music on my ears. I was able to understand Japanese after two months and could speak the language after three. There are sounds utilized in the Japanese language that are never even heard in Western languages. Although my vocabulary is still not extensive, most Japanese are quite surprised at my accent, which they say is authentic and nonforeign.

Most tourists in Japan have a difficult time with the food. Japan is not all tempura and sukiyaki, common Japanese dishes found in the West. Either the looks of certain foods, or their contents are enough to turn many foreigners pale. Raw fish (*sashimi*), for example, which includes raw octopus, will make Westerners cringe. I actually saw one woman faint dead away after she was told that she had just eaten a piece of raw octopus. Ever since my first taste of sashimi, I was hooked (which might not be the best choice of metaphors when one speaks of fish). Other strange, exotic Japanese foods have so delighted my taste buds that I now must have Japanese food at least twice a week.

The scalding baths that Japanese bathe in, at times reaching one hundred and twenty degrees, became a daily staple for me after my first dip. I was one of the few tourists to attend the public baths, still a great attraction in Japanese cities. I found that the atmosphere of hot bathing combined with small talk was a most effective way of easing tired muscles at the end of a busy day. After one of these baths a masseur can be easily found—the Japanese way of assuring a good night's sleep. My frequent bouts with insomnia disappeared during the four months spent in Japan.

I adapted to every aspect of Japanese life immediately and with ease. The Japanese, completely aware of the difference between Eastern and Western customs, go out of their way to make a foreigner feel at home. They were usually surprised and sometimes baffled by my ability to conform to even the "strangest" of Oriental ways. Nothing was strange to me, for while I was in Japan, I had the impression that I had done everything before. To me, it really wasn't adaptation, but rather a recalling of that which I had once experienced. The most far-out elements of Japanese life afforded me both comfort and joy.

My trip to Japan was a four-month *"Déjà-vu"* experience.

CHAPTER III

In addition to the Miyajima incident, other happenings occurred in Japan that confirmed my belief in my own reincarnation. One such event took place in Tokyo, at the temple-residence of a Buddhist priest, Bungo Ozawa, of the Nichiren-shu sect.

Bungo is extremely intelligent, devoted, and sensitive; most important, he is a joyful man, who also happens to be interested in psychic phenomena. He had read about me in a Japanese magazine article that my interpreter Ryuske Tokunaga had written after our first meeting several years ago, while Ryuske was a visitor to New York City.

When Bungo discovered that I was about to embark for Japan, he wrote and asked that I spend some time with him. I went to Bungo's temple more than once and spent many hours there in meditation and happiness.

To enter into Bungo Ozawa's vibration is an experience one doesn't forget very easily. He is the only being I have ever met who wears a perpetual expression of joyfulness on his face. Whatever he is involved in—talking, eating, listening—Bungo's smile never leaves. His inner peace and contentment are forever apparent in those permanently upturned corners of his mouth. Constant bliss—I think this is what religion is, and should be (see Plate 11).

While I was in Tokyo, Bungo celebrated the birthday of the temple he presided over and invited many of his friends and relatives to a pleasant gathering. Among them was the Kurayoshi family, consisting of a mother and two sons.

I met the Kurayoshi family at the temple on several different occasions after that night. One particular afternoon, we sat around the low mahogany table, on the tatami-grass-matted floor, in the tastefully appointed living quarters of the temple. We sipped *o-cha* (green tea) and ate *sushi* (rice balls topped by raw fish and seaweed), looking out onto a tranquil miniature garden, replete with a shimmering pond stocked with *koi* (carp), and dwarf pine trees. The eldest of the Kurayoshi sons reached over to me and asked if I as yet did not remember him.

Ryuske translated the question, and, naturally, I thought that Mr. Kurayoshi meant in the recent past, possibly on a trip he might have made to the United States.

Mr. Kurayoshi clasped my hand, at the wrist, and executed a strange handshake, from side to side, unlike anything I had ever seen. Staring straight at me, he again asked the question. The vibrations set up by this exchange fired the atmosphere and almost knocked me over—kind of an electric shock.

Mr. Kurayoshi explained that he had become aware of a time when he and I had been together before, in another existence.

As he spoke, a definite but strange feeling came over me. Although I could not say where, when, or under what circumstances, I knew that I had indeed encountered the soul, presently ensconced in the body sitting opposite me, prior to the current meeting.

Ryuske translated Mr. Kurayoshi's next impression. "He said that you will someday recall the time and place when you were together."

It had been decided on my initial visit to the temple that I should have a Japanese name. On a subsequent trip, Bungo presented me with a wooden doorplate that had been engraved with my new name in elaborate, calligraphic writing.

The name given me is *Kurayoshi Ryugen,* which literally translated means "Dragon Eyes." This, Bungo said, is symbolic of my awareness, the third eye. Also, legend has it that the dragon was the most perceptive of creatures.

The Kurayoshi family wished me to have their family name, the eldest son again reaffirming his feeling that we had been together before, in fact, as brothers.

"We will meet again, Daniel-san," were Mr. Kurayoshi's parting words. "You will be back in Japan, for the next phase of your work will be here in the East."

Unfortunately, I have not, as yet, been able to place Mr. Kurayoshi in any specific remembrance. Maybe I will have to go back to Japan before I can do that.

But, I, too, experienced much the same feeling as Mr. Kurayoshi when I first met Ryuske's aunt, his mother's elder sister. Both of the sisters presently live together on Japan's southernmost island, Kyushu, in the country village of Izumi.

In keeping with custom, she is called *O'va-chan,* a term of both deep respect and endearment afforded the elderly women of Japan. And how the elderly are honored and loved in Japan!

The village of Izumi and its surrounding environs had scarcely before been the host to foreigners, and although I was the one supposed to be doing the watching, in many cases I was the one being watched—though it was ever so subtle and non-imposing.

Izumi, like many villages on Kyushu, is a magnificent place to experience the Japan of yore, as it was hundreds of years ago. Terrace gardens, with their flooded rice paddies, rise up mountain slopes like giant water-filled footprints (see Plate 12); silkworm farms—the treasured worms, watched over as though they were precious jewels, are kept in rows of square boxes in darkened farmhouse living rooms during their period of hibernation; thatched-roof houses nestled in vibrant green valleys deeper than those of Switzerland; women washing or dyeing clothes and pieces of material in rushing streams; *o-cha* (green tea) leaves drying indoors on large wicker trays before they are sold at market. If the traveler goes only to the large cities of Japan and ignores the very distant towns and villages, he does not see the real Japan.

O'ba-chan lives in a typical, old, thatched-roof house. The immense size of its single room amazed me. Screens and sliding paper doors section off parts of the home as needed. The house is built high off the ground to provide for ground storage space as there are no basements in this type of home. In the center of the room is the dining table, the true nucleus of the Japanese home since the beginning of time. Mealtime in Japan borders on the ritualistic. The physical aspect of dining takes second place to the more important fact that this is the time when a busy family is brought together spiritually. It is a time of relaxation, a time of joy, a time of love. It is a refreshing counterpart to most Western homes I have been in, where mealtime becomes the hour in which to voice complaints, angers, and daily frustrations. During mealtime in America, more children have been sent to their rooms, more women have fled their tables in tears, and more men have left the house in anger, than at any hour of the day.

From the moment I stepped off the train in Izumi, a sympatico relationship between O'ba-chan and myself was established, an immediate feeling of kindred spirits. (Does any Westerner truly realize the meaning of that well-used expression?)

I think everyone has sometimes had the overwhelming feeling after being introduced to an absolute stranger that they somehow knew or recognized that person. It usually is most

1 LEFT Ryuske Tokunaga, my friend and interpreter

2 BELOW Itsukushima Shrine, built in the thirteenth century and gateway to the island of Miyajima

· 3 OPPOSITE UPPER LEFT A five-storied pagoda recalled from the past

4 OPPOSITE UPPER RIGHT In the corridors of the Itsukushima Shrine,
where I stop to meditate

5 OPPOSITE MIDDLE Ryuske pauses between the two massive bronze
lions before we pass through the torii gate leading to the
Itsukushima Shrine

6 OPPOSITE BELOW Japanese students asking for autographs at
Hiroshima

7 ABOVE The semi-tame deer of Miyajima

8 BELOW A private home now, this was a temple I remembered from
a previous life

9 LEFT Stone steps on Miyajima that I felt I had climbed as a Buddhist priest many centuries before

10 BELOW The stone wall I had psychically envisioned became a reality moments later

11 PREVIOUS PAGE ABOVE Bungo Azawa

12 PREVIOUS PAGE BELOW The flooded rice paddies of southern Japan

13 LEFT Midori Tokunaga and I on her wedding day

14 BELOW Ryuske's aunt, O'ba-chan, and I discover a Karmic bond

frustrating. Try as you may, you cannot place the person in your life experience. Mr. Kurayoshi had recognized me in this manner, and I, upon bowing my introduction to O'ba-chan, realized that I indeed had known her before.

O'ba-chan and I did not speak, except the few faltering words I knew of Japanese at that time. She did not know any English. We did not have to speak, we communicated on a second, deeper level. O'ba-chan knew when I was hungry, tired, or merely curious to learn something more of her town. Before I asked for anything, she instinctively realized what it was.

I too, was able to sense the depth of the anguish and unhappiness she had experienced in this life. Ryuske later confirmed the sad vibrations around this lovely woman. O'ba-chan had, many years ago, gone to Korea to start a business with her husband. For a while, they were most successful. Their business flourished and they had five children.

Without warning, O'ba-chan's husband contracted an incurable disease. He slowly and agonizingly went insane, becoming as a wild animal, violently mistreating his wife and family until the day he died. Anti-Japanese feeling, owing to Japan's growing militaristic and imperialistic state, was dominant throughout the rest of Asia. Everything O'ba-chan owned was confiscated, and she had to gather up the children one day and make a desperate dash for her home country.

Three of the children died on the trek homeward, one from starvation. She reached her home town of Izumi exhausted, with half her family gone. The war machine of Japan was sending its fathers and sons to battle. And, as in all wars, it was the lower middle class, the majority of the nation, who suffer most. Ryuske's family went to Izumi to wait out the war, hoping to escape the fate of the factory and industrial cities.

Ryuske, who was a child of ten or eleven at the time, recalls going to market one day with his aunt. On the way home, American fighter planes dove at the villagers, who were on the dirt road, machine-gunning them at several different intervals. O'ba-chan threw herself over her nephew. They were lucky. Others were less fortunate.

One must take into consideration that this section of Japan is isolated countryside. There are no factories; no one even had a gun in those days. Many Japanese who experienced the war and its effects, sadly laugh at the current "exposé" of American military men involved in the atrocities of Southeast Asia. It happened twenty-five years ago, and probably before that. It has occurred throughout history, to all peoples involved in all wars. America has not cornered the market on massacres, nor are massacres an American invention.

Following the war's end, there was little in the way of food or goods on Kyushu. Everything had been taken and utilized by the Japanese military in the last futile months of the war. There were no chickens, cows, crops, or rice. O'ba-chan, her sister, and their families ate leaves from the trees and grass from the hillsides to fight off starvation. Some of them made it.

O'ba-chan, a deeply religious person, has transcended the material circumstances of her life. I knew that she was aware of Karma, being a Buddhist, and that she knew the disasters in her life were Karmic: debts she had built up in previous lives she was now paying back, beautifully and lovingly. I know that I have been with her in at least one of those lives, and I know that I will be with her again. When we accept the theory of reincarnation, avenues of awareness and sensitivity of those we come into contact with open up continually.

Back in the United States, through meditation, I realized that O'ba-chan had been my mother in a previous life. A photograph taken in her ancient farmhouse clearly shows not only the Oriental physical changes of my face, which occurred while I was in Japan (and which are evident in all the photographs taken there), but the kinship between a mother and son as well (see Plate 14).

There were not only definite facial changes that took place but many mental and spiritual changes as well. In the short time I was in Japan, unconscious reflexes and actions—I believe to be owing to a former life there—caused me to be more Oriental than Western.

There is another aspect of my reincarnation discovery in

Japan. I first became aware of it in the ancient fishing resort city of Gifu. I had been invited there to attend the wedding of Ryuske's brother Yukio.

Gifu is famous for its cormorant fishing. On spring and summer nights, fishing boats, laden with visitors, put out onto the Gifu River. Shining black cormorant birds attached to lengthy pieces of cord dive for river smelt. The cord around their neck prevents them from swallowing the fish. They bring one up onto the deck, deposit it, and then commence with the entire procedure again. At the end of the catch, each bird is rewarded with several pieces of fish. The main part of the catch is cooked and eaten on board by the guests. It is quite festive, and there is much singing and rejoicing.

Yukio Tokunaga is one of the managers of the main resort hotel in Gifu. His bride-to-be Midori also worked in the hotel, and that is how they met.

Midori is of the traditional school of Japanese women. Her natural beauty, shyness, charm, and understanding of the human element are without peer. She is also an unsurpassed cook and creates most of her own clothes.

Midori went out of her way to make sure that I was completely at ease and comfortable in her hometown of Gifu. I was at first embarrassed by her attention, until I found that it is the custom for guests in a Japanese home to be considered first, even before the head of the house. There was no jealousy from Midori's husband-to-be. In fact, he encouraged her hospitality to me.

If it rained, Midori would open her umbrella over my head. If I came to a door, Midori welcomed me inside. When I emerged from an automobile, Midori would run around, open the door, and assist me out of the car! I realize that ladies from women's lib movements would have heart attacks about all this but, no matter. Midori was not in the least bit subservient, and I know she didn't feel taken advantage of. She loved being a Japanese woman at all times in every way. Although it appears to outsiders that men rule their women in Japan, I observed that Japanese females got more of their demands and wishes simply by remaining as female and enchanting as possible. One simply has to reciprocate their kindness, attention, and completely feminine manner. You of women's lib, stick that in your pantsuit and wear it.

Believe me, if Midori had not married Yukio, I would be in pursuit of her at this very moment (see Plate 13).

I had a kimono made for their wedding. The marriage ceremony was beautifully performed in a fantastically elaborate sanctuary. It is rare that foreigners are asked to the most private ceremony of marriage in Japan, but by this time Ryuske's family, especially his mother, had accepted me as one of their own—as an older brother.

Ryuske's mother Hiroko and I communicated through ESP. We kept reading one another's thoughts, and that's a bit difficult when you realize that each of us thought in a different language. She knew of my inner feelings about her daughter-in-law-to-be and sympathized with me. After the wedding, Hiroko would always give me a nudge when she felt a girl of Midori's caliber was present.

Several weeks before the marriage took place, Ryuske had said that some of the guests would entertain at the reception after the ceremony.

"Why don't you sing?" he suggested.

I thought it over and decided that I would do a Japanese song. Listening to the radio, I chose one that was catchy and a bit modern. Ryuske wrote the name of the song down. We went to phonograph shops, listening to many versions of the song, until we found one that was an orchestra rendition played (almost) in my key.

Ryuske transliterated the words into phonetic Roman syllables. I learned them in three days. At the reception, I sang the number. The response was tremendous. In fact, for the next few weeks, I had to sing the song wherever I went. When we left Gifu and arrived in other towns, those members of the Tokunaga family and their friends who had not been to the wedding would ask that I sing the song. My "fame" preceded me.

Everyone was quite surprised. Not that I could sing, almost everyone can sing well in Japan, but that my pronunciation was so good and that the Japanese spirit I incorporated into the expression of the song was perfect.

And I must say that it was far easier for me to get up and sing in Japanese than it is for me to do an American song, and that includes the times I had to sing professionally when I was in the theater. Again, I attributed this to a past life in Japan, the unconscious knowledge of which enables me to "become" Japanese at times.

At first I thought it was merely the overwhelming politeness of the Japanese people that made them praise my little song so highly. But I was to find out differently. If and when I so desire it, a career in Japan awaits me—as a singer! Businessmen and others involved in show business in Japan have offered me opportunities to come back to Japan and to do television shows and make recordings, singing Japanese songs. Knowing the keen business acumen of new Japan, I realized that this is more than politeness.

Because of my ability to adapt to any Japanese situation and because my expression of self becomes Japanese, I am still called *hanna gygiin* (strange foreigner) by many Japanese, especially the younger generation, who cannot understand the whys and wherefores of the Japanese spirit that lurks somewhere inside me. I know what it is, as does O'ba-chan, the Kurayoshi family, Ryuske's mother, Bungo Ozawa and a few others who recognize that I am somehow, in some inexplicable way, Japanese.

CHAPTER IV

While I was in Tokyo, I frequented a certain foreign-periodical bookshop on the Ginza, which is Japan's answer to Fifth Avenue in New York City. Browsing through the available books, I came upon a copy of *The New English Bible—With the Apocrypha*. I was instantly drawn to it, although I am not very Bible-minded. Having been born a Catholic, I did not have the opportunity, as a child, to read the Bible properly, nor to understand its various layers of interpretation. Also, I must admit, much of what I read in the Bible at a later time turned me off. I thought the Bible somewhat pretentious, a bit far-fetched, and too laden with symbolism for the common person to comprehend.

For some unexplainable reason, however, I was impelled to purchase this new version of the Bible with the Apocrypha. It was the second Bible that I ever had in my possession. My thought was to reread it to see what its teachings might offer that I had not gotten from them before. Until that time, I had no idea what the Apocrypha was, nor could I even pronounce it. To my surprise, the Apocrypha not only complemented what I was learning on my Oriental journey, it also enhanced my new ideals. Was it a coincidence that I had been led to the Apocrypha while I was in the Orient? Or, as the Eastern teachers believe, was it that when one becomes ready for the next spiritual step, the path is made clear?

The Apocrypha are writings that are so highly evolved, of such an important and precious nature that only the initiates and the highest order of clergy in early Christianity could have access to them. *Apocrypha* is a Greek word that means, in literal translation, "the hidden." They are made up of fifteen chapters that were originally found in the Greek Bible, the version most commonly used by the early Church.

Parts of the Apocrypha can be found dispersed throughout both Greek and Latin manuscripts of the Old Testament. They were not collected into a separate book of their own until A.D. 1520. With the exception of the Second Book of Esdras they are all in the Greek version of the Old Testament, the version created for the Greek-speaking peoples of Egypt. They were accepted as biblical by the early Church and were quoted as Scripture by early Greek scholars and writers. The Apocrypha were never utilized in the Hebrew Bible and were eventually removed from the Greek version by those in the hierarchy who felt that the people were not spiritually or mentally prepared for certain aspects of the Apocrypha's contents.

The Second Book of Esdras was the least used and was even purposely left out of many versions of the early Bible that included the First Book of Esdras. I became intrigued. Why was this book treated in the manner that it was? What did it contain? Why was it "hidden" from the people? I discovered the answer.

The Second Book of Esdras contains much that is prophetic for our times, the latter part of the twentieth century. It is also replete with countless implications relating to reincarnation.

Unsure of my conscious interpretation, I did some deep meditation on the Apocrypha; meditation comes easy in the peaceful and beautiful countryside of Japan. The atmosphere is conducive for enlightenment.

Both the First and Second Books of Esdras are about Ezra, who has his own book in the Old Testament. Ezra was a direct descendant of a chief priest, Aaron. He was a scribe of the times and had been taught in the law of Moses. He had been a visitor to Jerusalem a number of times, sent there by the king of the period to spread his teachings and to measure the religious temper of the people. He was disappointed in the materialism that he found.

Ezra was a prophet and was indeed psychic. Through astral projection he was able to see into the future. At one point, he clearly states that in a vision he saw "a man in white robes, surrounded by others like him, coming down from a mountain" —this I take to mean Jesus Christ and the Sermon on the Mount, although it was not to occur until a much later time in history.

Fearful of what he psychically knew and sensed for the people of his time and those yet to come, Ezra became very meditative and in semitrancelike situations, he was able to communicate with what is described as an angel. The name given the angel was Uriel. You might say that Ezra confronted a spirit, or an entity. My own psychic impression is that he was dealing with his subconscious mind, which afforded him this enlightenment. The Second Book of Esdras consists of "meetings" between Ezra and Uriel and the exchange that took place.

I do feel that there are more Apocryphal (hidden) books of the Bible and that they will come to light as they are needed. It is no coincidence that there has been a recent upsurge of interest in the Apocrypha.

I have not taken the writings of the Apocrypha in any specific order but rather as I was directed to them in my meditations and only as they pertain to either reincarnation or predictions for our era. My psychic evaluations of these writings are in the brackets you will find within the quotes.

During one of his deep meditations, Ezra asks Uriel, "Why have the people you loved been put at the mercy of godless nations? Why has the law of our fathers been brought to nothing, and the written covenants made a dead letter?"

Uriel answers, "The present age is passing away. The evil is sown but has not yet been reaped. Until the crop of evil has been reaped, until the ground where it was sown has vanished, there will be no room for the field which has been sown with the good." [This is a reference to the current age, the age of Pisces, which is passing away. This age has been sown with the evil seeds (materialism) and not until the age of Aquarius will the good seeds (spirituality) that are being planted be able to sprout. The nations (or, more directly, the governments in command at the present time) must vanish before the good can flourish.]

Ezra asks, "But when? How long have we to wait? Why are our lives so short and miserable?"

Uriel continues, "Do not be in a greater hurry than the Most High Himself. You are in a hurry for yourself alone; the Most High for many." [Ezra was thinking of himself as having only one life and was expressing his impatience with the suffering and pain that each person experiences in the one life he has to live. Uriel says that the Most High is regarding not only Ezra's present life but his past and succeeding lives yet to be lived.]

Uriel continues, "You are asking the same questions that are asked in the storehouse of souls [where the souls stay between earthly incarnations]. They wish to know how long they must stay, when will they get their just reward [advance to a higher level of existence and not return to earth]. They are told that they can do so [advance] as soon as the number like themselves is complete. The world has been weighed in a balance, and the ages have been numbered and measured; nothing will be moved, nothing will be altered, until the appointed number is achieved. [Every soul has a certain number of incarnations that it must experience until it learns the lessons and pays the Karma; nothing, not even the Most High, can alter that. The appointed number of lives needed to fulfill the Karma must be achieved.]"

Ezra asks if there will be any signs that the appointed number of ages has been reached, when the new world spoken of will come to pass.

Uriel answers that there indeed will be signs to foretell the changing of the ages, from the material into the spiritual. In so doing, Uriel is speaking of our own present age. "There will come a time when the inhabitants of the earth will be seized with panic. The way of truth will be hidden from sight, and the land will be barren of faith. There will be a great increase in wickedness, worse than anything you have now seen or have ever heard of. The countries you now see governing the world [the United States, China, Russia] will become as trackless deserts, laid waste for all to see. After the third period [measuring the time of Egyptian history as the first period, the Age of Christ as the second, and Western civilization as the third, which is coming to an end] you will see confusion everywhere.

"The sun will begin to shine in the middle of the night [the blinding sunlike rays of atomic weapons]. Trees will drip blood, nations will be in confusion, and even the courses of the stars will be changed. [These are the effects of atomic weapons; the earth will be knocked off its axis to such a degree that those on it will have a slightly different perspective of the heavens above.] Chasms will open [earthquakes] in many places and spout fire. [Lava from the earth's bowels will explode from the chasms.]

"A king, unwelcome to the inhabitants of the earth, will succeed to the throne; even the birds will fly away. [The governments of the countries leading the world at this time will topple, and the revolutionaries who will take over will be more unwelcome and cause more suffering than the governments they will depose.] Wild beasts will range far afield [wandering from shock of the extensive bombing that will occur], women will give birth to monsters [radiation effects], and fresh springs will run with saltwater [owing to the explosions, the earth's water levels will shift, causing this phenomenon], and everywhere friends will become as enemies. Then, understanding will be hidden and withdraw to her secret chamber. Many will seek her but not find her. The earth will overflow with vice and wickedness. One person will ask another if any justice has passed his way. Or any just man. And he will answer, 'No.' In those days men will hope, but hope in vain; they will strive but not succeed."

Ezra pleads with Uriel, "But surely, what you say is for those who are alive at the end of the world. What is to be the fate of those who lived before us, or of ourselves, or of those yet to come?"

Uriel answers, "I will compare the judgment to a circle; the latest will not be too late, nor the earliest too early." [The circle is symbolic of reincarnation—no beginning and no ending. Those born at the beginning of time will be there at the end; it will not be too early for them, for they will also be the latest, through the process of incarnation. In actuality, they are one and the same.]

Uriel further delves into areas of reincarnation. "Put your question in terms of a woman's womb. Ask a woman, if she can give birth to ten children, why does she not give birth to the ten at one and the same time? Why do so at intervals?"

Ezra says that the births must come at intervals. Uriel responds with, "True, and the earth's womb is to bring forth, at intervals, those already conceived in it." [Souls created at the beginning of time will be incarnated at intervals.]

Uriel imparts more of the signs that will signify the end of the current age. "Listen, the time shall come when the signs I have foretold will be seen; the city which is now invisible shall appear, and the country now concealed be made visible." [This is a direct reference to the rising of Atlantis.]

Uriel continues, "How terrible the sight of what is coming from the East! [China] Hordes of dragons will sally forth with countless chariots [missiles with atomic weapons], and from the first day of their advance, their hissing will spread across the land, to fill all who hear them with fear and consternation.

"A time will come when food will grow cheap, so cheap that people will imagine they have been sent peace and prosperity. But, at that very moment, the earth will become a hotbed of disasters—sword, famine, and anarchy. The earth will be left almost empty, and its cities in ruin. For out of a whole city, only ten [from out of a hundred] will survive; in the countryside, those left will be found hiding in the holes and the rocks. The earth will be left a desert, and the fields will be overrun with briers; thorns will grow over the roads and paths, because there will be little life to tread them under.

"Girls will live in mourning with none to marry them. Women will mourn because they have no one to support them. The young men who should have married them will be killed in the war, and the husband wiped out by famine." [In the preceding two paragraphs Uriel explains that there will be a short period of a false peace, but that it will not last. The country, China, will come forward offering herself as a friend but will have devious intentions all the while. At the height of this seeming friendship, China will strike out in a fashion unheard of in history. This will be the final confrontation of nations.]

Uriel says that "All labor shall be labor in vain. Their fruits will be gathered by foreigners [invaders from enemy countries] who will plunder their goods, pull down their houses, and take their children captive. Any who make money do so only to have it plundered.

"The more care lavished on their cities, houses and property, and on their own persons [the more material we become at the expense of progressive spirituality, the more we will have to pay] the fiercer will the indignation against them be. But, in a short time, wickedness [materialism] will be swept from the earth, and the reign of justice over us will begin." [This signifies the start of the age of Aquarius, the thousand years of peace predicted by seers and mystics.]

Uriel gives "a warning to Asia" [China and Russia], saying that "Asia has become like Babylon," interested in power, material wealth, and splendor and compares this unspiritual desire to that of "a whore who dresses up to attract new lovers" [the lovers being other, smaller countries being lured toward the supposed splendors of communism]. Uriel continues, "Asia has copied all the schemes and practices of a vile harlot. Therefore, terrible evils will befall you—poverty, plague, violence, and death. Then you will be a poor weak woman, bruised, beaten, and wounded, unable to receive your lovers anymore."

Uriel says that "the Most High would not be so fierce with Asia had she not murdered the chosen ones [the people who inhabit the countries of Asia, who did not follow current ways and were slaughtered]." The punishment would not have been so severe had Asia not "gloated over the blows struck the people." When they, therefore, begin the great war, they will suffer the most. Uriel explains exactly how. "For strong is his arm who bends the bow, and sharp the arrows which he shoots; once they are on their way, they will not stop before they reach the ends of the earth [a reference to guided missiles]. Calamities are let loose and will not turn back before they strike the earth. An arrow [missile] shot by a powerful archer [missile launcher] does not turn back; no more will the calamities be recalled which are let loose against you. [Missiles that will be so perfected that they cannot be intercepted by antimissile weapons will be utilized. They cannot be stopped before striking a given target.]

Uriel then tells Ezra that the Most High has pleaded with the earth people as a father with his sons, as a mother with her daughters or a nurse with her children. "Has the Most High not said, 'Be my people and I will be your God? But now what am I to do with you? When you offer me sacrifice [material offerings, meaningless prayers, the vast riches of the churches—all at the expense of spiritual evolvement] I will turn away from you.'"

Uriel then tells Ezra that the Most High has said that He sent His servants, the prophets, from the beginning of time, "'but you took and killed them. I will hand over your homes to a people soon to come [the following generations], who will trust me, though they have not known me [because they had not been taught by their unspiritual parents], who will do my bidding, though I gave them no signs; who never saw the prophets and yet will keep in mind what the prophets taught of old [the turning of the young toward the ways of spirituality by their own desire]. I vow that this people yet to come shall have my favor. Their little ones shall jump for joy. They have not seen me with their eyes, but they shall perceive by the spirit [through psychic awareness] and believe all that I have said.'"

Uriel leaves much hope for the coming generations, who will recognize their spiritual value. I, personally, have never thought of myself as a "prophet of doom," and after having received in meditation the explanation of the Apocrypha, I became quite depressed about the dark picture that it seemed to paint for the future. Also, I somehow detest preachers, and under no circumstances do I wish to be known as a "scare-the-hell-out-of-'em" preacher type.

But I feel that one does not have to be psychic to perceive the gross materialism, the hate, the unloving vibrations that presently engulf the major cities of the world. But I feel as Uriel, or Ezra's subconscious, that this time is passing away; further, that there must be a culmination of the destructive vibrations now on the earth. I see the disasters ahead as not the death of the earth plane, but as a rebirth. Birth of any kind is violent, and that is the reason we are going through this period.

Materialism will be thrown off, but this will not be accomplished easily. Hopefully, the difficult lessons ahead of us will serve to guide those who will be reincarnated into a new era of spiritual enlightenment. Already, I perceive the desire for spiritual attainment in the young, who are beginning to turn away from material crutches such as drugs. We must, and will, go through the predicted catastrophe, but after that, we will indeed have an age of peace, brotherhood, understanding, and love. The sooner we accept this and work toward that "glorious time" the shorter the period of hatred and violence. It is up to each of us, as individuals and as nations, to assist in ushering in, with haste, this New Age, this "thousand years of peace."

CHAPTER V

I returned from the Orient an implicit believer in the theory of reincarnation. How could I refute what had occurred in regard to my own awareness of a past life? However, coming back to live in Western civilization somewhat dampened my enthusiasm and uncovered doubts that must have been deep within the intellectual part of my mind. Perhaps, I began to think, I had let my imagination and emotionalism, combined with the Oriental atmosphere, run a bit wild. And several persons to whom I related my experiences acted more than a bit skeptical.

I had to find out if there was justification in the skepticism and open mockery one finds prevalent in Western man's thinking concerning reincarnation. After all, I was going to utilize the supposition of "many lives" in the psychic consultations I would give.

The Apocrypha had greatly assisted me in overcoming Westernized, Christian thinking, but I realized that additional evidence was needed to quell the uncertainty I would be confronted with when I made known my new beliefs.

With a feeling akin to fear—the fear of discovering that I was wrong—I probed into what the great minds of the world, past and present, had felt about reincarnation. I had hoped that they, in their infinite wisdom, might offer me either concrete evidence of continuing life or at least afford me the inspiration to continue on the path of this new-found philosophy.

I have always had recurring thoughts, nightmares if you will, of being labeled a "weirdo" or a "fanatical occult freak"; the stand I was now going to take might just transform this fear into a reality. I had been accepted as an "authentic" psychic— but reincarnation? That would be an entirely new avenue of credibility in my work that would have to be accepted.

I need not have worried. The data that I soon amassed, substantiating my own new theories of rebirth, were awe-inspiring and staggering in both quantity and quality. The material collected—what the world's most learned men have thought, said, or written on the subject—could fill a book of its own. I will, therefore, quote barely a minimum of the most valid information I gleaned from these august and eminent persons.

From the earliest times, man has believed in an afterlife and a return to this world. Even the cave writings of prehistoric man show evidence of this. Uncovered in the archaeological diggings of ancient Egypt were many of the works of Hermes. In his writings, this lofty Egyptian left the legacy of reincarnation that has taken hold through the centuries and is still practiced and believed by a major portion of the world's population: "From one Soul of the Universe are all souls derived. When one strives to know God and to injure none, then that soul becomes divine; such a soul eventually becomes a part of the all intelligence. The impious soul, however, punishes itself by seeking a human body to enter into. No other body can receive a human soul; it cannot enter the body of an animal devoid of reason. The soul passes from human form to human form, the mansions of its pilgrimage are manifold. Thou art from old, Oh, soul of man—yes, thou art from everlasting to everlasting."

The Egyptians were the first people to set up and teach a doctrine of belief in several "sheaths" or *bodies* of man. They contended that there was, first, the *Ka* "the divine, continuing spirit of man"; the *Ab* "the intellect or will of man"; the *Hati* "the vitality or energy of man"; the *Tet* "man's astral body that can travel at will"; and the *Xa* "the physical body of man."

It was on the banks of the Nile that most of what is taught today about the soul and its rebirth had its beginnings. The Persians took the fundamental beliefs about reincarnation from the Egyptians and elaborated upon them. Teachers were able to educate their people on a much higher scale than even the Egyptians.

The most renowned of the many "occult" teachers in Greece was Pythagoras, who openly taught his students the doctrines of reincarnation. This teaching—which resembles the Hindu understanding of reincarnation—aspires to show its pupils that there are, as was taught in Egypt, several "sheaths" (bodies) of experience in each being and that the higher part of man's nature (the soul) survives physical death and continues, while the lower sheaths (the physical and emotional) perish.

Pythagoras taught that after death, the higher part of the soul passes on into a "region of bliss" (a divine school, if you will) where it receives knowledge and feels the beneficent influence of developed and advanced souls. In this way, the soul is being equipped for a new life, which gives it an incentive to strive for a life with higher values than the last one. This "region of bliss" is merely a probation period, and the soul must eventually step down to another incarnation.

Situations and experiences in the new life were thought to be determined by the actions, thoughts, and mental tendencies of former lives. It is further believed that Pythagoras was the first teacher-master to introduce the law of Karma into the realms of the occult—of course, it was not known by that name at the time.

Pythagoras said that he had recall from other lives. When visiting the temple of Hera, Pythagoras, it is recorded, recognized a shield that hung from the wall. The shield had belonged to the warrior Euphorbus and had been carried by him into the battle of Troy. Pythagoras said that he was the reincarnation of Euphorbus and that he could recall much of the siege of Troy.

Plato, another respected, immortal Greek, offered many truths based on the theory of reincarnation. In his *Book of Laws* Plato made this statement: "Know that if you become worse you will go to the worse souls, or if you become better, to the better. In every succession of life and death, you will do and suffer what like may justly suffer at the hands of like."

Aristotle, yet another eminent Greek philosopher, also believed that man's soul continued. "There are generated in the earth, plants, and all living creatures, and in the whole universe, an animal heat; insomuch that in a manner, all places are full of souls."

Another example of Aristotle's teachings, as found in his treatise entitled *De Generatione Animae* is: "The soul of man is immortal, and can perform its proper functions without the help of any terrestrial body."

Tenets of reincarnation can be found in the ancient cultures of China. Early Chinese mystics and seers practiced a form of belief in rebirth. Lao-Tze, China's most profound sage, taught the workings of reincarnation to his inner circle of pupils and adherents. He taught that the human soul was composed of different parts: the *Huen* "the spiritual principle" and the *Phi* "the semi-material vital principle." Together, these two parts cause the body to act and animate it.

Lao-Tze said, "To be ignorant that the true self is immortal is to remain in a grievous state of error, and to experience many calamities by reason thereof. Know ye, that there is a part of man which is subtle and spiritual, and which is the heaven-bound portion of himself."

Lao-Tze taught that the *Huen* persisted in existence throughout countless incarnations, returning to the higher realms of existence only when it had completed its round of earth-life experiences.

In the beliefs of Taoism, it is taught that the deeds, good and evil, that a person commits in a present life will bear fruit in future existences.

The civilization of Rome, like our own, was unfortunately involved in material advancement at the expense of the spiritual; this proved to be its downfall. However, even in that most material of eras, there crept into everyday life thoughts on reincarnation.

In one of the works of Cicero, the prominent Roman wrote: "Know that it is not thou, but thy body alone, which is mortal and will perish. The individual in his entirety resides in the soul, and not in the outward form."

Ovid, the Roman poet, compiled many verses that indicated his belief in a continuing existence.

The Emperor Julian, nephew of Constantine the Great, believed that he was the reincarnated soul of Alexander the Great.

From the beginning of their culture, the people of India have not only believed in but have put into everyday practice the teachings of rebirth. The wondrous Hindu Bible, the *Bhagavad-Gita,* clearly states the Hindu belief of rebirth. "The man whose devotion has been broken off by death, goeth to the regions of the righteous, where he dwells for an immensity of years and is then born again on earth. Being thus born again, he comes in contact with the knowledge which belonged to him in his former body and from that time he struggles more diligently toward perfection. The person who, striving with all his might, obtaineth perfection because of efforts continued through many births, goes to the supreme goal."

Also, in the *Bhagavad-Gita,* one of the characters says, "There never was a time when I, nor thou, nor any of these princes of earth was not; nor shall there ever come a time, hereafter, when any of us shall cease to be. In other incarnations, the soul shall live again, and move and play its role. The body may die, it may be slain, it may be completely destroyed, but the soul that has occupied it remaineth unharmed.

"As a man throweth away his old garments, replacing them with new and brighter ones, even so the dweller of the body, having quit its old mortal frame, entereth into others which are freshly prepared for it. Many have been my births and rebirths, Oh Prince, and many have been thine own. But between us lies this difference—I am conscious of all my countless lives, but thou lackest remembrance of thine."

Down through the ages, India has offered much insight into the concept of "many lives." In modern times, the beloved and world-respected teacher-master Mohandas Gandhi delved into the ideas of reincarnation. He once said, "The form (material body) ever changes, ever perishes. What is said about rebirth is sound. It is nature's kindness that we do not remember our past births. Where would the good be in remembering in detail the numberless births we have gone though? The present life would be a burden if we carried such a tremendous load of memories. If death is not a prelude to another life, the inter-mediate period is a cruel mockery."

Few people know that in Tibet all the monks are not called lamas. *Lama* is a crowning name placed on those who live the most saintly of lives and who are able, because of the higher level they have reached in soul understanding, to recall past lives. There is documentation that these monks can commu-nicate with other members of the same sect regarding previous lives when they had been together, offering each other elaborate details on those lives.

When one advances in Judaism, he comes to study the *Cabala* ("secret writings"), which contain many references to the nature of the soul, its past, present, and future existences. There are several outer coverings to the writings of the *Cabala,* which means that it can be interpreted on seven different levels. It is further taught that the key to each level lies within the awareness of the soul attempting to break through the next layer. Through the process of reincarnation, if one has applied himself in a former life, the key to the understanding of the next level is given him in the present life. To those who do not progress, the key may never be presented.

In the book of Zohar, Volume II (a book in the *Cabala*), one comes upon this statement: "All souls are subject to the trials of transmigration [rebirth of the soul]: and men do not know the designs of the Most High with regard to them: they know not how they are being judged, both before coming into the world and when they leave it. They do not know how many transformations and mysterious trials they must undergo; how many souls and spirits come to this world without returning to the palace of the Divine King, the Most High.

"The souls must reenter the absolute substance whence they have emerged. But to accomplish this end, they must develop all the perfections, the germs of which are planted in them; and if they have not fulfilled this condition during one lifetime, they must commence another, a third, and so forth, until they have acquired the condition which fits them for a reunion with the Most High."

In Mohammedanism, the *Koran* deals at length with the possibility of rebirth. "And when his body falleth off all together, as an old shell, his soul doeth well by the releasing, and formeth a new one instead. Ye who cry when ye go out of this body, wept also when ye were born into it. . . . The person of man is but a mask which the soul putteth on for a season; it weareth it for a proper time and then casteth it off, and another is worn in its stead. The Spirits which now have affinity shall be kindred together, although they all meet new persons and names."

Many of the great writers of Western civilization tended to believe and put into their writings theories on reincarnation. Both H. G. Wells and Rudyard Kipling (possibly because of his Indian experiences) utilized the teachings of reincarnation in their work. Yeats, the immortal Irish poet, studied the writings and teachings of Madame Blavatsky, the theosophist who believed that the soul comes back.

Sir Arthur Conan Doyle, creator of Sherlock Holmes, was vastly interested in spiritualism and related psychic phenomena.

In his work, *A History of Spiritualism,* he wrote, "Such existences [through reincarnation] of the soul may well form a cycle which is all clear to us when we come to the end of it, when perhaps we may see a whole rosary of lives threaded upon one personality. The doctrine of Karma, of the apparent injustice of any single life, are arguments in its [rebirth's] favor, and so perhaps are those vague recognitions and memories which are occasionally too definite to be easily explained as atavistic impressions."

Reincarnation has escaped no country, not even Russia. In what is probably the greatest novel of all time, *War and Peace,* Natasha, one of the leading characters, says, "I feel that a person goes on remembering and remembering, until one can recall what happened before the present life." A bit later, Natasha continues: "The soul is immortal, so, if I am to live forever, I have lived before too, I have lived for all eternity. . . . There will be today, and there will be tomorrow, and there will be forever, and yesterday has been and the day before."

It is amazing to find such interest in reincarnation in a Communist country.

My favorite novel, *Dr. Zhivago,* was written by the often-suppressed Boris Pasternak. In one part of the book, Dr. Zhivago is consoling Anna Ivanovna who has almost died and who has said that when one is about to die, it is the terror of not knowing of the hereafter and not the actual loss of life which is so overpowering. Dr. Zhivago gives her this response: "But all the time, life, one, immense, identical, throughout its innumerable combinations and transformations fills the universe and is continually reborn. You are anxious about whether you will rise from the dead or not, but you rose from the dead when you were born and you didn't notice it . . . There is nothing to fear. There is no such thing as death. Death has nothing to do with us . . . What we need is something new, and the new thing is life eternal."

In modern psychiatry, Carl Jung wrote, "The mere fact that people talk about rebirth, and that there is such a concept at all, means that a store of psychic experiences designated by that term must actually exist."

In his *Letters and Journals,* Henry David Thoreau wrote, "I lived in Judea eighteen hundred years ago, but I never knew that there was such a one as Christ amongst my contemporaries. As the stars looked to me when I was a shepherd in Assyria, they look to me now as a New Englander. As far back as I can recall I have unconsciously referred to the experiences of a previous state of existence."

Thomas Edison said, "The unit of life is composed of swarms of billions of highly charged entities which live in the cells. I believe that when a man dies, this swarm deserts the body and goes out into space, but keeps on and enters another cycle of life and is immortal."

The early Christians did believe in some form of rebirth. In the Bible, when one reads Matthew 11 and 17, one finds Jesus actually telling his disciples that Elias will be the reincarnation of John the Baptist. "And as they came down from the mountains, Jesus charged them, saying, Tell the vision to no man, until the Son of Man be risen again from the dead. And his disciples asked him, saying, Why then say the scribes that Elias must first come? And Jesus answered and said unto them, Elias truly shall first come and restore all things. But I say unto you, That Elias is come already, and they knew him not, but have done unto him whatsoever they listed. Likewise shall also the Son of man suffer of them. Then the disciples understood that he spake unto them of John the Baptist [who was already dead]."

And so it goes, on and on, quotes from the writings and statements of those who have led the world in science, philosophy, art, and religion. And yet the majority of intellectual Westerners still doubt that there is reincarnation, still tend to laugh it off, and still prefer to walk in the dark when the light is constantly with them and simply needs to be switched on.

I have come to the conclusion that most people who have investigated the theory of reincarnation and reject it are actually afraid of it. For if they were to accept the precepts of

Karma, there would be no excuse whatsoever for them not to surrender the material aspects of their existence that they, for some reason, desperately and foolishly hold onto and are so fearful of losing.

Are you one of the fearful who are walking in the dark? Then why don't you just reach out and turn the light on? If I have but made you cognizant of the possibility that there is re-incarnation, then I have succeeded in my work. You see, I am completely aware of my own Karma. . . .

INTRODUCTION
TO ASTROLOGY

Ever since man appeared on earth, he has shown interest in
the stars and planet constellations that glimmered in the skies
above him. Cavemen left hieroglyphics recording their interest
in the heavens.

In the earliest times of human gatherings, people began to
take note that certain physical, mental, and personality characteristics would reoccur in different persons who were born
in specific times according to whatever calendar then followed.
A study of this was undertaken by the Egyptians, then by the
Babylonians. These peoples honed and refined what was to become the first astrological system.

Later, when Westerners discovered astrology, they not only

had to translate the astrologic teachings but had to adapt them to their own calendar as well, losing something in both the translation and in the utilization of a different calendar.

In the original Egyptian and in other Oriental astrologic systems, Karma played a most important role. It was believed—and in the higher realms of Oriental astrologic teachings it still is—that astrology is a means in which a record is kept, a Karmic record. In other words, it is no accident that a person is born on a specific day, in a certain year. Those characteristics and traits, physical or mental, that are conducive to each astrological sign, will afford the soul being born at that time an assurance of confronting certain Karmic debts. For example: I was born under the Western astrological sign of Taurus the Bull. The characteristics of Taurus, such as stubbornness and anger, are Karmic in nature, attributes that I somehow let get the best of me in a previous lifetime possibly under another sign. By being born in Taurus, I am assured that I will have the same aspects to confront and will have opportunities to overcome them. There would be no way to escape them, their being an integral part of the sign.

The West tends to disregard reincarnation as an important part of astrology. In Japan, the astrologers I talked with seemed to think it is a most important aspect. My psychic impression is that astrology is a kind of filing system, where "those in charge" are able to keep tabs of some kind. Heaven may be a bit more organized than we believe.

The only Western astrologer I know of who utilizes reincarnation in her work is the lovely soul, Linda Goodman. She has had opposition from other astrologers because of this, but her work has more meaning and insight than does that of the majority of astrologers.

It is imperative for me to state at this point that Oriental astrology does not intrude upon, contradict, or denounce Western astrology. It is simply more definite and accurate and much more specific.

In the Orient, astrology plays an important role in everyday life, whether it be in business or in the home. Persons born in Japan have gained influence in their positions (even high governmental stations) because of favorable signs. Born under unfavorable astrological signs, some Orientals have not been able to progress in their work. Marriages often occur with the astrological signs of the bride and groom taken into consideration. Perhaps this accounts for the low divorce rate in the Orient.

Interviewing various Oriental astrologers and those Orientals interested in astrology, it was difficult for me to discover the secret of how they calculate their system. It seems that much of the calculative knowledge is kept hidden, handed down from generation to generation. This is by no means selfish; rather, it is felt that astrology is a lifetime study, and to pass on calculative information in a helter-skelter manner could be most destructive. There is an easy chance of miscalculation and misinterpretation. This, therefore, is not a self-calculative astrology book; rather it is an introduction to your Eastern star, the Oriental astrological sign under which you were born.

When I was a youngster, I recall being taken to a Chinese restaurant for a birthday celebration. When our waiter asked my mother my birth date, she obliged. He stopped for a moment, figuring out something in his mind.

"Ahhh," the waiter groaned, "your son was born in the Year of the Rat!"

When one is an American child and is told that he was born in the Year of the Rat, he can become very upset. I don't particularly like rats, so I didn't pursue the subject for that reason.

Later, I checked out Oriental astrology and discovered that it too had twelve basic signs, like its Western counterpart. Each of the signs was named after an animal, and some, such as the snake, seemed even more repulsive to me than the rat.

When I went to the Orient, I found out that the designated animal names of the twelve signs did not mean that one was like his sign physically or mentally. I was happy about that; I still don't like rats.

The naming of the various animals in Oriental astrology is traced back to legend. Although the system was in practice long before the civilizations of China and Japan, the signs had different names. It wasn't until the time of Buddha that the names of animals were utilized in Oriental astrology.

Buddha's life came to an end beneath a gingko tree, while Buddha was in deep meditation. Buddha had lived a major part of His life under this tree, teaching and spreading the words of His wisdom.

Just before He made the transition from His earthly body, having spent His life communing with nature, an important part of His philosophy, Buddha sent out telepathic thoughts to the animal kingdom. Some animals received His message and came forth to pay homage to the departing One.

In all, twelve animals came into the compound, and they arrived in this order: the rat, the ox, the tiger, the rabbit, the dragon (lizard), the snake, the horse, the sheep, the monkey, the cock, the dog, and last but not least, the boar.

For their respectful homage, each of the animals was rewarded by having one of the twelve astrological signs (and corresponding constellations) named after it. This is as acceptable to me as Jesus walking on water, Moses parting the Red Sea, and dozens of other so-called legends attached to various religions.

If you cannot believe that the twelve animals came on their own into the compound, it might suffice to say that these animals happened to be in the vicinity of the compound at the time of Buddha's transition. (I prefer the legend.)

Although Eastern astrology has twelve different signs as in its Western counterpart, these signs do not represent the twelve months of the year as they do in Western astrology. Each sign is representational of a specific year in a twelve-year cycle. When one twelve-year cycle is completed, another begins, with each year named after an animal, again repeated in the same succession as they appeared to Buddha during one of his final earthly meditations.

We will not start with the initial year in which the first cycle began. Instead, we will use the year 1900 as a basic commencement point. It happens that 1900 was the Year of the Rat, the first animal sign to appear in any given cycle, marking the beginning of a new twelve-year cycle.

To follow through, 1901 would have been the Year of the Ox; 1902 was the Year of the Tiger; 1903 was the Year of the Rabbit; 1904 was the Year of the Dragon (lizard); 1905 was the Year of the Snake; 1906 was the Year of the Horse; 1907 was the Year of the Sheep; 1908 was the Year of the Monkey; 1909 was the Year of the Cock; 1910 was the Year of the Dog; 1911 was the Year of the Boar. The year 1912 would then start a new cycle, being the Year of the Rat.

If you wish to discover the sign of someone born in any specific year, start counting either forward, if that person was born after 1900, or count backward (Rat, 1900; Boar, 1899; Dog, 1898; Cock, 1897, etc.) if they were born before 1900. Each year being an animal sign, when you come to the year of the person whose sign you are seeking, whatever animal you have ended with is the Oriental sign of that year.

Having found the sign, now turn to the specific month in the particular year in which the person was born. It is as simple as that. If it were March 10, 1911, you would have been born in the Year of the Boar. You are then called a March Boar Year person. Since there are twelve months in each of those years, by multiplying we find there are one hundred and forty-four different Oriental astrological signs.

When you realize that there are so many signs in the Oriental astrological system, you find that it is more specific than the twelve signs of Western astrology, even in a primer such as this book can only hope to be.

In Japan, the astrological system has been made to coincide with the Western calendar, the one now widely used by the Japanese. That was most fortunate for me in my work of getting this into English, as the true Oriental calendar is somewhere in the year forty-five hundred, not in the nineteen-hundreds.

Remember, it is not by chance that you were born in the year and month you were. Because of Karmic aspects and experiences that your sign will afford you, your soul was placed in its present body and came onto the earth plane accordingly.

I—*The Year of the Rat*

1900
1912
1924
1936
1948
1960
1972

IV—*The Year of the Rabbit*

1903
1915
1927
1939
1951
1963
1975

II—*The Year of the Ox*

1901
1913
1925
1937
1949
1961
1973

V—*The Year of the Dragon*

1904
1916
1928
1940
1952
1964
1976

III—*The Year of the Tiger*

1902
1914
1926
1938
1950
1962
1974

VI—*The Year of the Snake*

1905
1917
1929
1941
1953
1965
1977

VII—*The Year of the Horse*

1906
1918
1930
1942
1954
1966
1978

X—*The Year of the Cock*

1909
1921
1933
1945
1957
1969
1981

VIII—*The Year of the Sheep*

1907
1919
1931
1943
1955
1967
1979

XI—*The Year of the Dog*

1910
1922
1934
1946
1958
1970
1982

IX—*The Year of the Monkey*

1908
1920
1932
1944
1956
1968
1980

XII—*The Year of the Boar*

1911
1923
1935
1947
1959
1971
1983

There will be certain aspects, good and bad, you will not recognize as being part of your character or personality. Possibly, you have thrown them off before reading this. And other traits found under your Eastern star might have been ignored or buried beneath the surface. As in Western astrology or in any mystical study, you, as an individual, have the power of choice to accept or deny any traits of personality herein. I have decided not to point out the Karmic aspects of each sign, other than to utilize them in a general manner. I am sure you will recognize them if they are a part of you.

I have found this system to be far more accurate for my family, friends, and myself than Western astrology. I hope you get as much out of it as I have.

One last word—the editor of this book, Joni Ebans (who is more Oriental than she suspects, expressing attributes of gentleness, kindness, and understanding in her approach to work that can and usually is materialistic and brutal), pointed out one major flaw regarding Eastern astrology.

"Daniel, what about all the Westerners who don't wish to have their ages known," Joni said. "It might be hard for them to give freely of their actual birth year."

If that is the case, and you are hesitant about giving your actual birth year, then make sure you skip twelve years, which would also be your sign twelve years later.

There are general characteristics of each animal sign at the beginning of the twelve different Oriental astrologic signs.

It is noted that persons born in the month of January of each sign are on what might be described as a "cusp," possessing attributes of the preceding sign.

An index covering the month and year of the Oriental astrological calendar appears on page 221.

THE YEAR OF THE RAT

General Traits

Persons born during the Year of the Rat are most intuitive. In fact, many of them possess one or more of the various aspects of extrasensory perception. They are also most inventive and creative. Rat Year persons have a venturesome spirit. There is a tendency for the Rat Year person to be jealous, especially in matters of love. Rat Year persons are the most charming of the Oriental Zodiac. They are very easily angered and can sometimes be quite tiresome to those around them.

The Year of the Rat—January

Those persons born in the month of January during the Year of the Rat exude a natural kind of overconfidence because of a most enthusiastic nature. Others, however, see them as coming on a bit too strong. The vibrations of this overconfidence will lead to difficulty for the January Rat Year person if he does not learn to control it.

Under the most trying conditions, January Rat persons will not show any signs of anger or of being upset. They are able to maintain their composure and keep their calm even when becoming involved in an automobile accident.

January Rat Year persons have their major success in business usually after the age of thirty-five, not before. Occupations best suited fot them would be in the fields of engineering, architecture, and medicine (they make excellent doctors or nurses).

Women born under this sign are very sociable and extroverted. However, they rarely give in to temptation. They are able to show control when any such temptations arise.

January Rat persons are highly influenced by the preceding sign, the Boar, especially December Boar, and should read the aspects of that sign as well, for they may fit into that category. This is what might be called a "cusp" sign in Western astrology.

January Rat persons learn by their bad experiences. Through difficult times, they acquire stability, something rare in the human condition.

Generally, January Rat persons have good relationships with anyone born in the year of the Ox, Rat, or Dragon. Males born under this sign should marry an October Ox or a March Rat female. Women of this sign do best with a January Ox Year male.

Persons born in January of a Rat Year should not ever marry anyone born in the Year of the Horse.

The Year of the Rat—February

Persons born in the month of February during the Year of the Rat have a very pronounced extrasensory perceptive ability. If a February Rat Year person tells you that the day is going to be a bright, clear one, filled with sunshine, even though it is pouring down rain when they tell you this, it will usually turn out to be the kind of day the February Rat Year person predicted.

Not only is their sensitivity extremely pronounced, but they usually act upon their ESP feelings rather than on any logical or intellectual explanation of the situation at hand. They are almost always correct in their predictive capacities. There are times when they lose this cycle of psychic awareness, which causes them to lose their pace of life as well. During this time, disaster will strike at the February Rat Year person.

February Rat Year persons cannot work methodically toward a goal. They must use their sensitivity and impulsiveness. They become very upset when they see others around them using methods and well-laid plans, taking the situation step by step to attain fulfillment or to reach a goal.

February Rat Year persons do quite well in occupations where they can utilize their sensitivity and their sophistication —fashion design, interior decoration, hair styling and the like.

The February Rat Year male is attracted to complacent, feminine types; he desires a woman who can keep and run a perfect household. A February Rat Year male usually chooses a woman who is very wise in these matters. He loves his mate passionately and does not wander.

The February Rat Year female has beautiful skin and can attract men more easily than women of most other signs, even other Rat Year women.

The best match for a February Rat Year male would be a September Sheep Year female.

The most acceptable marriage for a February Rat Year female would be with a December Horse or July Dragon Year male, or those men born in any month during the Year of the Monkey.

Both males and females of this sign should be careful of relationships with those persons born in the Year of the Snake.

The Year of the Rat—March

Persons born in the month of March during a Year of the Rat are very aggressive, at least outwardly. Within themselves, however, they are doubtful and very complicated. One should not be put off by a March Rat Year person's active aggressiveness.

March Rat Year persons tend to be "loners" and should seek employment in jobs where there are not too many other people around them. If there are many confusing vibrations around them, March Rat Year persons become upset and act in an untypical manner.

It is most difficult for a March Rat Year person to say no to another person. He tries his best to be affirmative, no matter what the situation. It is for this reason that a March Rat Year person must be careful. This is not the basis for a good friendship, and many people will take advantage of the March Rat Year person's inability to say no. In many cases, a good friend of the March Rat Year person will break his fortune.

March Rat Year persons must not introduce their lovers or fiancés to their close friends; if they do, they are liable to lose out on their romance. There is a tendency for close friends of March Rat Year persons to fall in love with their lovers or fiancés.

March Rat Year persons have a most changeable life when it comes to economics—constantly up and down, never stable. Sometimes they are flush, and at other times they have nothing. They are never in the middle of the road when it comes to money matters. They must learn to control themselves in their spending; no matter how well they are doing, it is wise for a March Rat person to save as much as possible for the financial dry season that inevitably comes to him.

March Rat Year persons are best suited for careers as gallery owners, small shop owners, fashion consultants, and auto racers (Jim Clark, the well-known racer, is a March Rat Year person, as are other famous racing-car drivers).

Females born in March of a Rat Year should pair off with March Snake or January Rat Year males. This sign is very well suited for their tastes. They must never marry the first-born male of any sign, including that of March Snake Year. This marriage would be a disaster. Dog Year Males (all months) make good companions for females born in a March Rat Year.

Males born in March of a Rat Year should marry a May Horse Year female. Other good relationships would be with August Dog or September Tiger women.

The Year of the Rat—April

Persons born in the month of April during the Year of the Rat give others a feeling of self-confidence, though within themselves they are most insecure. They also have a tendency to appear much older than they really are, either because of their looks or their actions.

They calculate everything they do before they act. Their psychic ability is very pronounced, and with a bit of development, they can forecast correctly for others. The occult is a good field of endeavor for them.

In their lives, they have many hits but rarely a home run. In other words, they may have countless small successes and accomplishments but hardly ever strike it big. They must forge on step by step. Nothing is ever handed to an April Rat Year person; they must work for whatever they are to realize.

At least once in his life, an April Rat Year person feels a terrific urge within himself to strive toward an artistic goal. He has a feeling that he can become a famous artist, writer, or performer and will work toward this goal, putting everything else aside during this period. Usually, he has a modicum of success at this, but it is indeed rare for him to reach great heights of achievement.

April Rat Year persons must be careful not to act too quickly or they will make unfortunate mistakes and ruin whatever it is they are attempting to do.

Persons of this sign make good government officials, teachers (especially math or physics), and scholars. Some areas of the occult are good also. April Rat persons do very well in their own business.

Females of this sign usually have beautiful hair and are attractive. They also possess a high degree of logic.

April Rat Year persons need romance in their lives. They fall in love easily, sometimes just out of the need to be loved. However, April Rat Year persons usually have only one major love in their life.

Females of this sign do best with a male who is born under the sign of the December Dog Year, as these men are very romantic. They also do well with May Horse Year males.

Males born under this sign should marry an August Rabbit female as these women are usually delightful and very sociable. They also do well with August Snake Year females.

Marlon Brando (April, 1924) is a typical April Rat Year person. He was able to forge ahead in a career that demanded self-confidence even though he was not known for this quality at the outset of his career. Marlon Brando also possessed the "older than looks" quality of an April Rat person. He is a true romantic and is said to be quite intuitive.

I must herewith admit that I am also an April Rat Year person. I cannot deny any of the information relating to this sign.

The Year of the Rat—May

Persons born during the month of May in a Rat Year are simple and direct. There is absolutely no artificiality about them. They are usually liked by other people because of their directness and simplicity and also because of their kindness, which they possess in quantity.

May Rat Year persons have grand ideals and hopes. They want to become prime ministers, presidents, or the like. However, if they are to bring this dream into reality, they must put tremendous effort into their work.

Females born under this sign tend to be a bit wild before marriage unless they curb this trait at an early age. They are attracted to places such as singles bars, ski resorts, discotheques —anywhere, in fact, where there is a lot of excitement and male companionship. Sexually, they can be most torrid. However, the closer they get to a friend or a partner, the more analytical and cooler they become as the relationship progresses.

May Rat Year persons can have many varied occupations. They do well by working for city planning or in city government capacities. They make excellent air controllers. They do well in the field of art. Philosophy, although mainly a soul-development process, can also be investigated by these persons as a field.

May Rat Year persons are very open. They feel that they have nothing to hide. They don't even shut out the light in their bedroom. They are clean to the very utmost, bathing quite often.

After marriage, women born under this sign are interested in the education of their children, almost to the exclusion of everything else.

Females born in a May Rat Year should marry September Dragon Year males. June Tiger Year males would also prove themselves in a relationship or marriage.

May Rat Year males would do well with August Ox Year females.

Persons born in May during a Rat Year should not marry anyone born in the Year of the Horse.

The Year of the Rat—June

Persons born in the month of June during the Year of the Rat are very kind and compassionate. They are also very speedy in any and all of their efforts. Their actions are not only quick, but usually done with an extra amount of cheerfulness. They love to laugh, and laughter is most important in their lives. In a group, the June Rat Year person stands out and is sometimes labeled a show-off.

In truth, the June Rat Year person does have a tendency to give an appearance of possessing more than he actually does.

He is likely to sew a "Made in Paris" clothes label on an inexpensive article of clothing purchased at a local store. This need to show himself in a more financially secure position will be the cause of his losing friends and could even be the one thing that will make him lose a chance at marriage.

June Rat Year persons have tendencies to argue with their bosses; though they may even be right in the argument, they should learn to control this, as they are apt to lose their job because of it. Usually June Rat Year persons do not like their jobs and do not become settled in an employment opportunity of their liking until after their thirtieth birthday.

June Rat Year persons love travel and therefore would do best working, for instance, for an airline (hostess, pilot, reservations clerk). They make very good travel agents or guides, and do well in other jobs related to transportation.

They also do well working in factories. Chemical factories are to their liking.

June Rat Year persons desire satisfaction of the mind more than they do sex. This is of most importance to them. However, in marriage, they usually choose the complete opposite of themselves—someone who is very physical and has strong sexual capacities.

June Rat Year males should marry February Monkey Year females, as they are quite steady.

Females should marry February Tiger Year or March Monkey Year males.

Men and women born in the month of June during a Rat Year must be careful of relationships with those persons born in the Year of the Boar and the Year of the Snake.

The Year of the Rat—July

Persons born in the month of July during a Rat Year show themselves to be friendly and gentle. Inwardly, they are strong. They tend to speak to others with a smile on their face, but inside they are not smiling. The grin may just be surface deep.

In their youth, July Rat Year persons are not too distinguished.

It isn't until their middle age that they rise to a better employment position. It is very difficult for a July Rat Year person to improve himself. For example: a salesman born under this sign may have a terrific sales record, but for one reason or another it is difficult for him to advance from sales into something better even though he has earned it.

July Rat Year persons can have good careers in secretarial work and accounting. If a man of this sign is well developed physically, he would be wise to seek a job as a bodyguard or bank guard. Women born under this sign make good social and welfare workers. They also have the ability to write.

Females inherit both the physical and mental aspects of their mother's side of the family. Males born in a July Rat Year tend to have mother fixations or complexes. They like large-breasted women. Even after marriage, men of this sign may seek relationships with other women. The wife of a July Rat male is usually quite nervous.

July Rat Year males should marry either July Sheep, June Tiger, or July Rabbit women. They also do well with September Boar women.

July Rat females are the ideal type for men of all signs! They do best themselves when they marry either an April Dragon or a February Horse Year male.

The Year of the Rat—August

Persons born in the month of August during the Year of the Rat possess vast knowledge and brain power. They are always in command of all their senses. If they enter a crowded bus, they can still find the one empty seat. They are most resourceful. However, there are times when these people make mistakes, sometimes to their great disadvantage, because of this cleverness.

Men born in the month of August during a Rat Year usually have a very fine record in school, often singled out as one of the intelligent ones. When they become a part of society, they are both aggressive and diplomatic. They also tend to be of the playboy type.

Women born under this sign are also extremely cheerful. Mostly, they have large eyes and very long, natural eyelashes. They admire the color red and wear not only red dresses but red accessories as well.

August Rat Year females can be quite matter of fact and usually do not care too much about sex. August Rat Year males, on the other hand, like to be creative in their sexual activities and can even be a bit sadistic.

Females of this sign would be wise to choose males born in February or June in the Year of the Cock. (These men have good economic outlooks.)

Males born under this sign are best suited for December Ox or March Dog Year females. They also do well with those women born in any month during the Year of the Dragon.

Occupations most suitable for August Rat Year persons are as copywriters, salesmen of home appliances, music teachers, and early-grade schoolteachers.

Both men and women of this sign should not marry anyone born in the Year of the Snake.

The Year of the Rat—September

Persons born in September during the Year of the Rat have highly developed mentalities. They are sensitive to other people's vibrations and utilize this sensitivity in their work or in daily living. They are most aware of and sensitive to other people's beauty as well.

They constantly strive to make improvements toward attaining the very heights of perfection. They are very hard on themselves and work to discipline the inner mind of their being.

September Rat Year persons have excellent memories and should seek employment where a good memory is of utmost importance.

The one major problem September Rat Year persons have is that they demand too much perfection of themselves and those around them. If they do not control this demand, they take a chance on losing much in their life.

September Rat Year males have a difficult time being understood by women. It is difficult for them to speak with women for this reason.

Persons born under this sign are able to make money. They are usually able to purchase their own house after only four years of marriage.

Females born in September of a Rat Year never chase men. They insist that the men in their life call on them. They will not telephone their men.

Occupations for September Rat Year persons should be in areas where their fantastic discipline could best be utilized. They do well as consultants, programmers, and letterers. They write well.

In love relationships, they tend to complain too much about their mate's bad points. There is difficulty in understanding their mate's way of thinking. Outside, however, they are able to express understanding with others.

Females born in September of a Rat Year are most honest. They also know how to satisfy their mates. September Rat Year females should marry June Sheep Year or February or October Tiger Year men.

The males of this sign should marry August Sheep Year females.

Truman Capote, the prolific writer, is a typical September Rat Year person (September 30, 1924). No one can question this man's mentality or sensitivity. In the books he has chosen to write there had to be tremendous disciplinary efforts in order for him to get the material (especially for *In Cold Blood*). He is said to be misunderstood by women and has certainly been able to make money, even at a young age.

Men and women born in September of a Rat Year should be wary of relationships with those persons born in either the Year of the Boar or the Year of the Horse.

The Year of the Rat—October

Persons born in the month of October during the Year of the Rat have a strong sense of the value of things. They are usually very brave. Quite intuitive, they hardly ever commit a wrong action.

October Rat Year persons should not work for other people if they can help it. Rather, they should start their own business. They are usually able to do this after they reach the age of thirty. When they do go into business, making money is not their main concern. The needs of their customers come first, and they treat their help well. Automatically, their business expands because of this correctly placed concern for those whom they serve. Whatever business they go into grows quite steadily.

October Rat Year males like girls too much. They tend to be very promiscuous, and this looseness in love matters will cause them to lose out eventually in social prestige.

Occupations best suited for October Rat Year persons are in dealing with food, whether it be food packaging or restaurants. They can even develop their own food products. Women of this sign make excellent cooks. In the field of art, October Rat Year persons make good sculptors. Females can knit quite well.

October Rat Year females usually find good husbands, but they are not satisfied and constantly look for a better man, having many affairs along the way. However, they will do everything they can not to hurt their husbands openly. October Rat Year women should, therefore, have three candidates for husbands before making their final choice. They should go with each man for at least a year.

October Rat Year males would do well to marry an April Monkey Year female. They should avoid at all costs women who are too outgoing, as this will prove to be bad for them later.

October Rat Year women should marry August Cock Year males. They also do well with any male born in the Year of the Ox.

Both men and women of this sign should not marry anyone born in the Year of the Horse.

The Year of the Rat—November

Persons born in the month of November during a Rat Year are very strong-willed. They know how to bring an idea to fruition, no matter how new or revolutionary the idea may be. They should be "the brains" of an organization and are most successful when they are.

Usually November Rat Year persons will decide everything in their lives by themselves, rarely taking advice. They should learn to listen to others more often. They must also learn to cooperate with their fellow men. They tend to be loners because of this personality trait.

November Rat Year persons are very talented. Their character, however, is so closed that they sometimes block their own talent.

Occupations for November Rat Year persons can be made in all the arts and crafts, dressmaking, and sales promotion. They usually have great success in business affairs when they are quite young and lose almost everything in middle age, only to gain it back in later years.

Both males and females of this sign are extremely well disciplined. They have very good memories, too.

November Rat Year persons look ultra chic and smart in their attire and know how to purchase clothes. When naked, however, they tend to be a bit heavy.

November Rat Year females should marry November Tiger, November Boar, or October Dragon Year males.

November Rat Year males do well with June Rabbit females.

Both men and women born in the month of November during the Year of the Rat should not marry anyone born in the Year of the Horse. They usually do not do well also with those persons born under their own sign, the Rat.

Toulouse-Lautrec (November 24, 1864) typifies the November Rat Year person. He was strong-willed and took advice from no one. His work in the field of art was indeed revolutionary, and he was a loner. His ideas were brought to fruition against all odds. He did do well for a period and then lost it all. He was said to be very disciplined and to possess an excellent memory.

The Year of the Rat—December

Persons born in the month of December during the Year of the Rat are the most typical of this sign. They are most charming, but tend to be fussy about small matters. Though they are able to maintain an outward show of control, they become angered quickly and easily.

December Rat Year persons have a great capacity for concentration. When they concentrate on a job, they don't tire as quickly as other persons do. They will work toward a goal without letting up, no matter what obstacles get in their way. They have great staying powers.

December Rat Year persons love to spend money on themselves. They do not like to lend money to others. They become generous only in a love relationship.

Persons born under this sign are quite impulsive and act accordingly. They love gossip about others.

Best occupations for this sign would be in the arts (theater especially), also in the fields of market research and copywriting. Women can arrange flowers and do needlepoint. They can perform elaborate jobs demanding great powers of discipline.

The December Rat Year male is very open in matters of sex and will talk to others about his prowess with lovers or even his wife. Females of this sign are also open in sexual matters. They love to be kissed on the neck and excite quite easily.

December Rat Year females should marry October Ox or November Dog Year males. They could also do well with a male born during any month in a Dragon Year except September.

The December Rat Year male would do best with a Monkey Year woman, any month.

Both males and females born in December of a Rat Year should not marry anyone born in the Year of the Horse or the Year of the Boar.

The great musician Pablo Casals is a typical December Rat Year person (December, 1876). His powers of concentration are renowned. He is said to be quite impulsive and is charming.

THE YEAR OF THE OX

General Traits

Persons born in the Year of the Ox are most gentle. They are usually very patient as well. Ox Year persons tend to be a bit eccentric. They have the capacity to inspire confidence in others. Ox Year persons are dexterous and work very well with their hands, especially where creativity is required. When angered, Ox Year persons can sometimes become violent or dangerous. They usually do not speak very much and will choose their words carefully. With a minimum of effort, Ox Year persons can be successful in their endeavors.

The Year of the Ox—January

Persons born in the month of January during the Year of the Ox have truly amazing powers of concentration. "If at first you don't succeed, try, try again" applies to them a hundredfold. They have the ability to repeat any effort many times until it is complete. They will pursue a course to the end and never give up.

January Ox Year persons have some characteristics of the previous sign, the Rat, and they should check out December of the Rat Year, for some of that month's qualities may pertain to them.

January Ox Year persons are very adaptable and make changes suitable to the atmosphere around them with little or no wear and tear on themselves. They adapt to any of the vibrations around them.

In many instances, January Ox Year people are born with artistic genius. They are indeed most creative. They have the ability to use each day as they would a canvas, painting it as they want it to be and then following through by living the day exactly as they had pictured it.

Individualism is another mark of the January Ox Year person. They do tend to be a bit too self-conscious. In areas of philosophy, religion, dress, and even food, these people cannot accept anything that they feel is not 100 percent a part of their character.

Yukio Mishima, the wonderful Japanese writer who committed suicide in 1970, was a typical January Ox Year person. He was adaptable to many modes of living, was born with artistic genius, and never gave up until a project was completed to his utter satisfaction. He was a true individualist, yet far too self-conscious. He was unable to accept the fact that the people around him were changing. He could not accept what he felt was a loss of spirituality in the Japanese people.

January Ox Year persons demand cleanliness in all things. If they see a speck of dirt in their food, they become upset, and sometimes the meal is ruined.

January Ox males handle their women with terrific mental control. Their love techniques are very refined. These men are excellent partners, but one shouldn't expect a good marriage with them. You cannot expect a real love with these men, for they are incapable of a lasting love.

January Ox females are usually not especially beautiful in a physical way; however, they possess lure and charm from within.

Males born under this sign should marry June Dog or January Rat Year females.

Females should marry September Dragon Year males.

Both men and women of this sign should not marry anyone born in the Year of the Sheep.

The Year of the Ox—February

Persons born in the month of February during an Ox Year are said to have "two faces." Their appearance and movements seem slow and labored. However, they can do anything they set their mind to. Others around them, even their own family, are always amazed at the accomplishments of a February Ox person.

February Ox persons are dreamers by nature. They are quite optimistic. Small upsets and problems do not bother them. In their dealings with others, February Ox Year persons feel that they are doing the right thing, but invariably, without knowledge or intent, they give those around them a hard time.

Classical music and paintings are very important to February Ox persons. They read quite a bit and dote on fine literature.

Usually February Ox persons have good fortune in life, but they must be careful; they can be easily cheated by unscrupulous people around them. Usually they have a good marriage. If they go into business with a partner, this too will be an affirmative relationship.

February Ox Year females enjoy gambling and love to play cards and go to Bingo games. This aspect is much stronger in the females of this sign than in the males.

Very favorable occupations could be made in interior design or poetry. In the field of art, February Ox people make exquisite tracers. Art design of any kind is good. February Ox Year persons also make good beauticians.

February Ox Year males like girls who are similar in character to Ophelia in *Hamlet*. (I'll let you figure that one out.)

Men should marry September Sheep Year females. They also do well with those women born in any month of the Year of the Snake.

Women of this sign get along best with an August Tiger Year man, but should not marry until after their thirtieth birthday.

Both men and women of this sign should not marry anyone born in the Year of the Dog.

February Ox Year females must be careful of stomach or liver ailments between the ages of twenty and twenty-nine. This condition could become serious if not taken care of in the earlier years of life.

The Year of the Ox—March

Those persons born in the month of March during the Year of the Ox are known by their independence. They desire to do everything by themselves. Usually, they are born with innate talents and possess physical strength more pronounced than in other signs.

March Ox Year persons cannot take criticism, even when they know that they are 100 percent wrong in a situation. Their family and friends must therefore be careful in offering a March Ox Year person any advice. Their good intent may be misconstrued and taken for criticism by the oversensitive Ox Year person.

March Ox Year persons keep matters of the heart guarded. They do not open their hearts to even their closest friends. When they are young, March Ox Year persons tend to have a most changeable life. They do not settle down till later years. They sometimes attain importance in their careers but only after terrific struggle and hardship in their endeavors.

Most March Ox Year persons cannot find a direction in life easily, and they should, therefore, strive to acquire a substantial base early in life. If they don't force themselves to have this base, they tend to squander their early years by drifting aimlessly.

These people should learn to listen to the advice of those above them in position, especially to their boss. If they do listen, March Ox Year persons will have success without the struggle they will have if they don't listen.

March Ox Year persons are best suited to occupations of free enterprise. They should be self-employed. They make excellent lawyers and doctors. They can also make a success in accounting.

March Ox Year men should marry July Cock Year women, as these girls are very intelligent and thoughtful.

March Ox Year women do best with September Snake Year males, as these men will offer advice that will be to their advantage. They also do well with November Dragon Year men.

Both men and women born in March during the Year of the Ox would do well to avoid involvements with those persons born in the Year of the Sheep.

Both males and females born under this sign have a tendency to develop asthmatic conditions. Allergies of many varieties are also a health problem that must be watched.

The artist Vincent Van Gogh (March 30, 1853) was a typical March Ox Year person. He carried his independence to the point of insanity and could not stand criticism. He was never able to find his direction in life. In his younger years, he was most changeable, and he did attain great importance in his career but only after vast struggle, hardship, and deprivation. He had no particular base in his early life and did drift.

The Year of the Ox—April

Persons born in the month of April during the Year of the Ox are strong-willed and possess a very keen intelligence. Their powers of concentration are absolutely breathtaking! They will concentrate on one thing until it is accomplished, never straying from their goal for a second. April Ox Year persons have secret desires to be powerful or famous. Because of their strong will and ability to concentrate, they can compete for the fame and power they want, usually winning.

April Ox Year persons tend to be quite masculine and have physiques like those of wild animals.

In their everyday life, April Ox Year persons are quite logical. They do not like to waste any time or labor. Males born under this sign are very interested in machines, especially automobiles. They are very good with plastic-model work.

Females born in April in an Ox Year are extremely intelligent and are also well disciplined. They are most sensible in the area of fashion. They are fastidious.

Occupationally, the April Ox person makes a good government official. He does well in all phases of politics. Men are excellent sportsmen. Females of this sign are also attracted to masculine jobs. They make fine leaders of women's liberation movements.

Both male and female persons born in an April Ox Year want mates that are of the same personality and character as themselves.

April Ox Year males should marry April Rabbit females.

April Ox Year females do best with April Ox or April Rabbit Year males.

Both men and women of this sign should not marry those persons born in the Year of the Horse.

The emperor of Japan, Hirohito (April 29, 1901), is a typical April Ox Year person. He has a most developed intelligence and his powers of concentration are said to be staggering. He has made a most noble emperor because of his awareness in matters of politics.

The Year of the Ox—May

Persons born in the month of May during the Year of the Ox are quite fortunate, for they are usually left a substantial inheritance. When it is said that a person was born with a silver spoon in his mouth, it most probably is a May Ox Year person that is being spoken of. If they don't inherit a fortune, they are usually able to make a great deal of money on their own.

May Ox Year persons are quite steady in character; but they tend to become a bit too optimistic, as so much seems to have been handed to them that they get used to a never-ending source of supply. When this source is cut off, as it sometimes is, a May Ox Year person finds it difficult to adjust.

May Ox Year persons should not change their jobs on a whim, for they will surely lose out.

Females of this sign tend to go way over their budget in spending, especially in matters of purchasing clothes. Both males and females born in May during an Ox Year must force themselves into moderation in all things.

May Ox Year persons should choose occupations with large companies that offer stable employment, such as electrical or construction companies. They also do well in any job dealing with jewelry, cigarettes, and gasoline. They can also be successful when working in any kind of area dealing in glass.

Males of this sign greatly admire physical beauty in their women. They will marry a woman merely for the sake of her outward beauty and do not ever give a thought to what might be beneath her appearance.

Females born under this sign desire intelligent men in their lives. They must continually be careful of what clothes they wear, for May Ox Year females are prone to catch colds.

Best match for May Ox Year males are July Tiger Year women.

May Ox Year females should marry August Rabbit Year males or a man born in any month during the Year of the Cock.

Both men and women of this sign should be careful of relationships with those persons born in the Year of the Horse or the Year of the Sheep.

The Year of the Ox—June

Those persons born in the month of June during the Year of the Ox have a dual personality. If they look intelligent and active, they usually are not. If they appear slow and unintelligent, they are the opposite. June Ox Year persons can stay in a room for hours studying philosophy, meditating, or reading deep, mind-expanding literature, and then they can suddenly jump into a high-speed sports car, dash off at great speed, and seek some physical adventure. Opposites come easy for persons born under this sign.

June Ox Year persons carry this duality over into most aspects of their life. If they place two records on a turntable of a phonograph, one may be a Beethoven symphony and the second a current hard-rock personality. Strangely June Ox Year persons rarely are aware of this duality and think it quite natural. June Ox Year persons are usually misunderstood for this reason, even though they make very loyal friends and are well liked when afforded the opportunity to become known.

A change in the way of life occurs for June Ox Year people in their middle forties. The results of this change can be either a plus or a minus, but they are always extreme. A great deal of the outcome of this change depends on previous efforts.

Careers best suited for these people are as writers and directors (especially for television); they also make good bankers and government officials.

In matters of love June Ox Year persons are very changeable. They can run either hot or cold, depending on which aspect of their dual personality emerges at a particular time. They are so changeable and varied that those associated with them, in business, as friends, or even in family relationships, have trouble getting along with them. They also have trouble remembering or keeping dates that they have made.

Both male and female June Ox Year persons are very jealous about their lovers or mates.

June Ox Year females should marry October Tiger males.

Males of this sign should be with July Boar or October Horse Year females.

Men and women of this sign do not do well with those persons born in the Year of the Sheep.

The Year of the Ox—July

Persons born in the month of July during an Ox Year are most mild-tempered. They are also very intelligent. They possess inner strength and have feelings that they are always right. No one can tell a July Ox Year person what to do.

July Ox Year persons sometimes cannot control the feelings that they are never wrong and are then accused of being egotists or at least of being too stubborn. They also lack stability and resent this quality when they see it in others.

They have a highly developed natural artistic sense, and after their middle age, this talent will bloom in the July Ox Year person as he becomes aware of the ability he possesses.

July Ox Year persons make wonderful musicians. Other occupations conducive to this sign are author, painter, and art director. They can also be most successful as social workers.

July Ox Year persons are forever aware of the etiquette of others around them. However, they tend to lack the good etiquette in their own home that they demand in others.

Stomach and eye diseases plague the July Ox Year person if he doesn't take special care with both these areas when he is in his younger years. He is also high-strung and must watch out for nervous disorders.

July Ox Year males should be with June Sheep Year females. They also do well with women born in any month during the Year of the Snake.

Females of this sign do best with December Cock Year males.

July Ox Year persons do not do well with those persons born in the Year of the Dog.

The Year of the Ox—August

Persons born in the month of August during the Year of the Ox are very sociable. They are also active in many diverse areas. Of all the signs, the August Ox Year person is the most broad-minded.

August Ox Year persons do not hide their feelings or emotions. They let you know exactly how they think and feel at all times. August Ox persons let "everything hang out." Few people are disappointed in their relationships with an August Ox Year person, for before they start a friendship, they know exactly what kind of a person they are dealing with. To quote a famous current comedian, "What you see is what you get!" Because of this complete honesty, other people are immediately and deeply attracted to August Ox Year persons.

People born under this sign are fine conversationalists and know much about many subjects. They love to be the host or hostess at a party. There is a desire for them to be in the spotlight at all times. People who are born in an August Ox Year attract and keep many friends, and are usually respected by everyone.

There is a tendency for the August Ox Year person to talk a little too much; he doesn't even hide the things that might best be kept secret. He should learn the old adage that, in some instances, silence is golden. Too much talk, whether it be honest or not, can prove to be the undoing of an August Ox Year person.

Occupationally, they make excellent announcers or masters of ceremonies. Cooking and all other phases of the culinary arts are very favorable, even wine tasting. They also could become successful singers if they so desired.

Both males and females of this sign tend to be aggressive sexually. And, after they fall in love, they discover the bad points in their lover's personality, and the love cools quickly, shocking the other party.

When they marry, August Ox Year persons should marry someone to whom they have been introduced by family or friends, rather than a person they have met on their own.

Males of this sign do well with May Boar or October Monkey Year females.

Females born in August of the Ox Year should marry April

Snake Year men. They also do well with men born in any month of the Year of the Rat.

August Ox Year persons usually do not have good relationships with those persons born in either the Year of the Sheep or the Year of the Dog.

The Year of the Ox—September

Persons born in the month of September during the Year of the Ox are noted for their great wit. They also have a wide range of knowledge. Another aspect of the September Ox person is his ability to handle other people.

When a September Ox Year person smiles, you know that the smile is sincere. He is very honest and rarely gives cause to be doubted by the many people who truly like him.

September Ox Year persons are blessed with the ability to love others as well as they do themselves. For this reason, they enjoy life to the utmost. Their distinguished social traits are inbred.

Financial sense and the capability of knowing how to save money are other attributes of the September Ox Year person.

Occupations for persons born under this sign can be made easily in the fields of printing, dyeing, architectural design.

At times, September Ox Year persons are too good to others and will lose out, because they don't assert enough of their own will in a given situation. Other people take advantage of the September Ox Year person's goodness and life-loving ability.

September Ox Year persons have fine memories and are very adept at imitating others.

In matters of the heart, they are both gentle and moderate. Usually, their love affairs and marriages run quite smoothly.

Females born under this sign are very constructive. They would do best marrying a January Horse or Dragon Year male.

Males born under this sign do well with September or February Rabbit Year or January Snake Year women.

Both males and females born in September of an Ox Year must be careful of relationships with those persons born in the Year of the Dog.

The Year of the Ox—Octobei

Persons born in the month of October during the Year of the Ox are extremely self-confident. They have big hopes, and ideals to match. If an October Ox Year person decides to do something, he will do it, no matter what obstacles are placed in his path or how long it takes.

October Ox Year persons have a desire to leave their parents' home at a very youthful age. This is a sign of their need for independence, which they will cultivate without letup and at all costs. It is also true that if a person born under this sign does indeed wish to be successful, he should leave home as soon as he can.

October Ox Year persons don't pay too much attention to wearing apparel or food; whatever there is, they will utilize. Because of their self-involvement they tend not to think about others. They must always work on human relations.

October Ox Year persons are utterly delightful when in the company of other people. They also will never break a promise once they make one.

If an October Ox Year person is to have a successful career, it MUST be in his own business. He should always be the employer rather than the employee! And the bigger the business, the better it is for him—trading companies, travel agencies, or virtually any kind of business that has connections across the oceans. Women make wonderful secretaries, especially those who are not married.

When they decide to marry, October Ox Year persons do so on the spur of the moment, shocking their family and friends. Their love affairs are usually simple and not too involved. They are not especially sex-oriented.

October Ox Year males should marry December Rat, December Dragon, or June Monkey Year ladies. They should NEVER marry September Dragon Year women, as there will be endless arguing and battling if they do.

October Ox Year females should marry April Dog or January Rat Year males.

A word of advice to anyone dating an October Ox Year person: don't leave the person born in this month for too long a period without some kind of contact, such as by telephone. If you do, you will surely lose that person.

The Year of the Ox—November

Those persons born in the month of November during the Year of the Ox are eminently strong-willed. They also tend to be cool and calm. Their planning ability, in most matters, is usually sensible. They are very distinguished although a bit selfish. They do not listen to others around them.

November Ox Year persons make fine leaders if they learn to widen their rather narrow viewpoints. Also, if they strive to become more sociable, they enjoy much more success.

Females born under this sign are markedly overcautious, especially in regard to men. They are very nervous when they have to confront males. This nervousness cannot be hidden when November Ox Year females are at a party or a dance where they are likely to be touched.

November Ox Year males make easy sexual conquests of women, as they have the rare capacity of allowing women to feel that they understand men.

Occupations should be made in the areas where there is much physical activity rather than scholastic endeavor. They are good managers in business and excel in sports. The November Ox Year person has the ability to become a specialist in agricultural affairs. They do very well in any aspect of machinery.

November Ox Year males have strong characters and should marry either January Dragon or September Cock Year women.

Females should marry January Cock Year men. Both men and women of this sign should not marry anyone born in the Year of the Dog.

Richard Burton (November 10, 1925) is a typical November Ox Year person. He certainly has strong will and gives a cool, calm appearance. His managers and the movie producers who have worked on his films will tell you that he has a tendency to make his own decisions. His sexual conquests are history and he is a most physically active man. To many people, Burton is an enigma, but it is said that his lovely wife understands him, or at least he lets her believe that she understands him.

The Year of the Ox—December

Persons born in December during the Year of the Ox possess the full effects of their sign and should read all the Ox-sign months, for their qualities are spread out among the various months.

Honor is of most importance to the December Ox Year person, even more than prestige or money. They cannot, however, stand to be beaten at anything and will also work to overcome any problems they may have in their life. They tend to become angry and lose patience when they are on a project and it is not going too well.

December Ox Year persons can adjust to circumstances surrounding them and will pursue a course of action with all their energies. They detest rumors—about themselves or others. In many cases, they would rather be dead than to hear untrue, unjust things that might be said about them.

The December Ox Year person has an immense feeling for humor and a lot of common sense as well, which stops him from becoming too wild.

In whatever occupation they are in, December Ox Year persons should progress one step at a time and not try to advance too rapidly. Females of this sign should think of having their own business after their children reach the age of eleven or twelve. They would be most successful in any business of their own. Both male and females of the December Ox sign make wonderful entertainers or sportsmen, where perseverance is so important.

It would be most wise for a December Ox Year person to marry someone who has the same kind of character or personality as himself. Before marriage, December Ox Year women tend to be introverts. They have an early distrust of men, and sometimes even a hatred. After marriage, they usually adjust and are able to throw off the bad feelings for men that they may have.

Males born under this sign do well with July Cock or November Dragon Year females.

Women born in December of an Ox Year should marry an August Rat Year male.

Both men and women born in December during the Year of the Ox should not ever marry anyone born in the Year of the Sheep.

Sammy Davis, Jr. (December 8, 1925) is a typical December Ox Year male. He cherishes his honor above all else and has worked to overcome the many problems in his life. Everyone knows the vast amounts of energy he uses in all his activities. His sense of humor is unquestionably one of the best of his time. He despises rumors about himself and others and will publicly denounce falsehoods that have been unjustly attributed to his friends.

THE YEAR OF THE TIGER

General Traits

Persons born in the Year of the Tiger are most sensitive. They are also extremely meditative and do much deep thinking. The implicit independence expressed by Tiger Year persons is usually interpreted as stubbornness by others. Tiger Year persons have a tendency to be suspicious and can sometimes be quite selfish. Courage is an attribute of persons born in the Year of the Tiger. In the Orient, there is a strong belief that a man who is born in the Year of the Tiger is indeed most fortunate, as it is the Oriental Zodiac sign of LUCK!

The Year of the Tiger—January

Persons born in the month of January during the Year of the Tiger can be said to be on the "cusp" of the previous sign, the Year of the Ox. They are quite delightful, if not too distinguished. January Tiger Year persons are a bit reserved in their relationships with others. In all their dealings, people born under this sign desire harmony. They are never "pushy."

January Tiger Year persons are very honest. They are not too flexible and find it difficult to bend in a situation, thinking only one way. They also feel that their way of thinking is easily understood by others. Much misunderstanding then occurs.

In working for a large company, January Tiger Year persons are gradually promoted. It is rare for them to get large promotions. They should align themselves with large, steady companies when seeking employment. Temporary work is bad for them.

January Tiger Year persons are not good conversationalists. They tend to ask quite inane, oversimple questions when meeting someone new: "Where do you live?" "Do you have a family?" "We are having nice weather, don't you think so?" Their questioning seems to be of a policelike nature. In fact, January Tiger Year persons would make fine policemen or -women.

It is indeed very difficult for a person born under this sign to express himself to others, especially when it comes to matters of love. He tends to lose out on romance because of this inability to make himself clear. They are therefore, to a great extent, loners. When they go out, it is usually to the movies, by themselves.

It would be most wise for a January Tiger Year person to marry someone who has the same kind of character as himself, as they can work on their lack of the social graces together.

Females born under this sign should marry September Rabbit Year or March Sheep Year males.

Males born under this sign do best with August Boar or September Dragon Year females. They also do well with those women born in any month during the Year of the Horse.

Both men and women born in January during the Year of the Tiger should not marry anyone born in the Year of the Snake.

The Year of the Tiger—February

Persons born in the month of February during the Year of the Tiger never rush into anything. Although they appear to be slow, once they make up their minds to do something, they are surprising in the speed with which they accomplish it. Those born under this sign learn almost everything they know in life through the process of experience, rather than by having been taught.

February Tiger Year persons move ahead on a slow but sure path, constantly making inroads toward set goals. They tend to have a problem with time and are very often late. They lose out on many things, because breaking a date or a promise does not mean as much to them as it might to others.

February Tiger Year females usually have beautiful skin, which tends to be moist. Males born under this sign dream a lot about the opposite sex. When they meet a girl, February Tiger Year males will imagine and contemplate exactly what kind of life the girl has. Males of this sign are very strong and tend to act tough.

February Tiger Year females keep a very good household. They can, and usually do, have a job on the outside as well. Women of this sign are not afraid to work very hard and will do so.

February Tiger Year persons have a tendency to marry their childhood sweethearts. They never marry unless they are sure that the other person completely understands them. They desire to have a home life and usually will create a good one.

February Tiger Year persons can work at almost any kind of job and rarely specialize.

Females born under this sign should marry November Horse, July Snake, or March Dog Year males.

Males would do best with a June or September Rat female.

Persons born in the month of February during the Year of

the Tiger should not marry anyone born in the Year of the Monkey.

A woman born in February during the Year of the Tiger usually has trouble a few years after her marriage, especially in the areas of finances and/or disease. She has a further tendency toward caring for her in-laws as well. Once she passes this age of anxiety and difficulty, she will be able to enjoy herself in later years. But there is a period that comes to a February Tiger Year female that is most difficult.

The Year of the Tiger—March

Persons born in the month of March during the Year of the Tiger are very sensitive. In fact, they have a tendency to be oversensitive. Their reactions to everything are quick. When they see something beautiful, March Tiger Year persons become too emotional.

March Tiger Year persons have a deep sympathy for the poor and others not as well off as themselves. They are usually the ones who will give donations to charities and other worthy causes without being asked.

Persons born under this sign surprise quite easily. It is said in the Orient that if you wish to play a practical joke on someone, choose a March Tiger Year person, as they make the best subjects for such a joke; their reactions are usually priceless.

March Tiger Year persons make superb actors and are especially adept in the field of social work.

The love in a March Tiger Year person's life usually grows out of a friendship. Before even thinking of sex, March Tiger Year persons will find and develop the things they have in common with their partner, such as hobbies, or sports.

Persons who have March Tiger Year friends feel that many secrets are being kept from them, which is not true.

In many instances, March Tiger Year persons will marry those who are similar in character to themselves but who come from entirely different backgrounds. There is a tendency for them to marry people born in far-off countries. There is usually an objection of some kind made by the March Tiger Year person's parents at the time of his marriage. But March Tiger Year persons should marry whomever they choose.

Females born under this sign do well with a February Monkey Year or a May Rabbit Year male as well as the July Tiger Year male.

Males should be with a January or May Rabbit Year or a July Dog Year female.

March Tiger Year persons should not marry anyone born in the Year of the Snake.

Tennessee Williams, the great American playwright (March 16, 1914), is a typical March Tiger Year person. The work he creates is that of a most sensitive man. From his writing one can tell that he is sometimes overwhelmed by beauty, be it spiritual or physical. He is concerned with those less well off than he is. Although he gives an impression of being aloof, possibly secretive, his friends claim that once known, he is really open and friendly. Mr. Williams is intrigued with foreign countries and is said to become infatuated with foreigners sooner than with his fellow countrymen.

The Year of the Tiger—April

Those persons born in the month of April during the Year of the Tiger are exceptionally cheerful. They are also radically independent. April Tiger Year persons constantly forge ahead in their efforts.

After their thirtieth birthday, April Tiger Year persons usually attain leadership status in their position. They have a desire to control the company for which they work and put all their energy into accomplishing this.

From their birth, April Tiger persons are most inquisitive. They like to investigate things and are always planning or thinking ahead. For these reasons, they make the best detectives.

In his line of work, as well as in his private life, the April Tiger person will not take any chances. Before he is thirty, he is most undistinguished. Greater importance falls upon him in middle years.

April Tiger Year persons love to eat. They always seem to be hungry. "Let's have a bite!" or, "I think it's time for lunch!" can be heard from the lips of April Tiger Year persons more often than from other people. Even after he has eaten, if you ask an April Tiger Year person to join you for something to eat, he will do so.

People born under this sign carry many things on their person; besides money, they are apt to have half a theater or movie ticket of a show they have seen months ago. They carry letters, expired lottery tickets, recipes, coupons and a host of other things.

April Tiger Year persons find it difficult to acquire or keep jobs that have much detail work or involve a lot of intricate technicality. Males tend to separate completely their business life from their home life.

April Tiger Year males should marry July Dog, February Snake, or October Monkey Year females. Those women can handle detail work very well themselves.

Women of this sign are usually tall, or have large physiques. When they marry, it is usually to a man taller than themselves. They should marry a June Dog Year or a January Cock Year male. A November Sheep Year man is also compatible.

Queen Elizabeth II (April 21, 1926) is a typical April Tiger Year person. She possesses both the cheerful and independent attributes of this sign. She did come into the leadership of her people a few years before her thirtieth birthday. Queen Elizabeth is said to be most inquisitive about dissimilar things and, in leading her people, she rarely takes any chances. I can't quite picture her as saying, "Let's have a bite!" but then, you never know. Queen Elizabeth is fairly tall and married a man much taller than herself.

The Year of the Tiger—May

Persons born in the month of May during the Year of the Tiger are usually the idol of their friends. They are cheerful and, physically, quite beautiful. The May Tiger Year person is usually the most important one in his circle of friends. He is a wonderful host at parties and makes the very best traveling companion.

Unusually kind, he sometimes finds it difficult to express this kindness because of basic feeling that he doesn't wish to impose on others. May Tiger Year persons have a tendency not to listen to others and to feel that they are always right. It is most difficult for a May Tiger Year person to keep to a schedule.

Persons born under this sign are said to be vengeful; and this is true, but only when the revenge is justifiable. It is also hard for May Tiger Year persons to show gratitude, for they are a bit too proud.

When May Tiger Year persons learn moderation, they become successful. They do make very good civil servants. In the Orient, many actresses were born during the month of May in the Year of the Tiger.

Males of this sign usually have extraordinarily beautiful physiques, and their movement is very much like that of a Tiger—smooth and cool. Girls are generally attracted to May Tiger Year males.

Women born in May of a Tiger Year should marry February Ox or May Snake Year males.

May Tiger Year males do well with either an August Snake Year or a February Dog Year female.

May Tiger Year persons should not marry anyone born in the Year of the Monkey.

Both males and females born in May of a Tiger Year should leave their parents' home at an early age. If by chance they must remain with their parents, they should keep their money separate. In fact, they should keep all household things, such as their kitchen, separate from that of their parents.

The Year of the Tiger—June

Persons born in the month of June during the Year of the Tiger act without thinking of rewards; they are, therefore, honest workers. A June Tiger Year person is able to express what he believes and will do so. His character is of a mild nature; he is not an extremist. In the majority of cases, parents of June Tiger Year persons were happy in their marriage and their children are well off for this. However, in cases where June Tiger Year children came from unhappy or broken homes, they are never able to overcome their background.

June Tiger Year persons have prestige in their life because of their personality and their honesty. Throughout their life, however, they have very high expenses and suffer because of this.

June Tiger Year persons tend to be scatterbrained. It is easy for them to fall asleep on a train or bus, awaken suddenly, and get off in a near state of panic. Usually, it is the station before or after the one that was their original destination. They will also leave their umbrellas on the train, their sunglasses at a Coke stand, and even their jackets or coats in theaters.

Females of this sign are most charming and have lovely foreheads and unusual voices.

June Tiger Year males chase after beautiful, voluptuous women. They go overboard with these women and stand a chance to lose a great deal by being too kind to them.

Females of the June Tiger Year sign should marry July Rat Year or February Sheep Year males.

Males do well with women born in any month during the Year of the Rat.

Both men and women of this sign should be careful of those persons born in the Year of the Boar or the Year of the Snake.

In the first six months of their marriage, females born under this sign suffer. They tend to be oversensitive and almost shy in the early stages of their marriage (usually one of the reasons their husbands were attracted to them in the first place). After a few months, however, they can become most aggressive. This, naturally, makes for trouble in a marital situation.

Marilyn Monroe (June 1, 1926) was a typical June Tiger Year female. Financial reward was not the motivation for her need to succeed. She was able to express her beliefs and her honesty. That is what made her a star and not the fact that she was a sex symbol, which unfortunately is what most people believe. Marilyn was never able to overcome her destructive background. She did achieve much prestige in her life owing to her personality and honesty. Everyone knows that Marilyn Monroe was scatterbrained, unable to ever be on time, forgetting everything behind. She was most charming and possessed a most unusual voice. From what we know of her marriages, the men seemed to be disappointed when, after several months together, Marilyn's shyness disappeared and a more aggressive nature came to the fore.

The Year of the Tiger—July

Those persons born in the month of July during the Year of the Tiger are considerably active. They have a most systematic way of thinking and planning things. By their sheer skill, July Tiger Year persons can live and survive very well in society. They usually have good jobs, make money, and do well in all other aspects of their lives.

If they are in a race, they remain in second place until just before the final stretch, when they will suddenly exert terrific power and strength, allowing them to come in first.

July Tiger Year persons hardly ever become fatigued or tired. They have the ability to change their mood completely, instantly. Even if they are standing in a moving train, they can close their eyes and sleep for a few moments.

After the age of forty, the July Tiger Year person must be careful for he can get into trouble in his business. This is not so much his own doing, but may be because of a mistake made by his secretary, assistant, or business partner.

Women born under this sign are WONDERFUL housewives. They also like to do social work or welfare activities.

Both males and females born in July of a Tiger Year usually marry people the complete opposite of themselves. They tend to admire the qualities their lovers have that they do not have, and vice versa. Separately, they each have so much to offer that their life together is varied, open, creative, and constructive. July Tiger Year persons are excellent parents.

Women born under this sign should marry May or December Ox Year or June Dog Year males.

July Tiger Year males would do well in marrying a May Ox Year or a March or November Tiger Year female.

Both men and women born in the month of July during the Year of the Tiger should not marry those persons born in the Year of the Snake.

The Year of the Tiger—August

Persons born in August of a Tiger Year are said to have a double personality. On the surface, they look and act very sociable, always gentlemen or ladies. Inwardly, the August Tiger Year person can be most independent and even selfish.

August Tiger Year persons have intuitivity (psychic awareness) but they never act on this alone, utilizing the other senses as well.

Females born under this sign can be narrow-minded. They should never go into schoolteaching.

The first marriage of an August Tiger Year person has a tendency to end up on the rocks. If this occurs, he marries again. The second marriage is usually a most happy one.

Both male and female August Tiger Year persons can get high by listening to music, making love, or utilizing their other senses, rather than indulging in drugs or alcohol.

Females of this sign usually marry a man from a different background than theirs. For example: an August Tiger Year female born on a farm will marry a city man, possibly a professional man.

August Tiger Year males are always punctual and are very precise in all matters. They expect and demand their family to follow. If they go away on a weekend vacation an August Tiger Year male sets the exact moment to leave and the exact moment to return, beforehand.

Women of this sign should marry December Rabbit Year or June Monkey Year males.

Men born in August of a Tiger Year do best with February Ox or May Boar Year women. Both these signs are easygoing, understanding, and flexible.

August Tiger Year persons must be careful of those people born in the Year of the Snake or their own sign, the Year of the Tiger.

The Year of the Tiger—September

Persons born in September of a Tiger Year are distinct stylists. They are the original "dandies"—even after their fortieth birthday, they like flashy colors and strong designs or patterns.

More importantly, there seem to be two completely different types born under this sign. One is very quick in his actions. The second is steady but slow in his progress. You will find both types born in a September Tiger Year. One thing they have in common is a great love of beauty.

At least once every month, the September Tiger Year person tries to quit smoking. In other words, those born under this sign make resolutions that they cannot keep.

Women born in September of a Tiger Year like to care for others, and they make good nurses. They are mostly moderate in their thoughts and actions and make better-than-average wives.

Males born under this sign are attracted to flashy women. At home, however, they are real babies, and therefore tend to marry wives who are motherlike in nature and attitude.

September Tiger Year males should marry April Snake Year or October Sheep Year females.

Women born under this sign should marry March Rat or February Tiger Year males. It is said that women of this sign desire strong men who will master them.

September Tiger Year persons should not marry anyone born in the Year of the Monkey.

Both male and female September Tiger Year persons must be on the alert for kidney disease, arthritis, and back problems.

The Year of the Tiger—October

Persons born in October of a Tiger Year have abundant good luck! They tend to be very fortunate indeed, having countless chances to improve socially and to become rich and famous. In their employment situation, October Tiger Year persons get excellent promotions. They marry outstanding husbands or wives. Of all the signs, October Tiger is the one with the most LUCK!

October Tiger Year persons tend to be too spread out in business matters. Whatever service they are in will grow so quickly that it becomes difficult to handle. October Tiger Year persons must consolidate; they should not be spread out too thin. At times, their luck in business is so good they tend to forget about it, thinking it will take care of itself as it has in the past. If they are not careful, they can lose the business because of those working for them.

Females of this sign have attractive eyes and should marry men who like to do household work. They are attracted to men with large noses, which means that October Tiger Year females had fathers who left a strong impression upon them, sometimes too strong, leaving them with the need to search for similar father types.

Women born in October of a Tiger Year should marry August Monkey, June Snake, or October Dog Year males.

October Tiger Year males do well with June Ox, September Rat, and December Rabbit Year females.

Both men and women of this sign must be careful of those people born in the Year of the Monkey.

Both the late Dwight D. Eisenhower (October 14, 1890) and the eminent Jonas Salk (October 28, 1914) are October Tiger Year persons. The success of these men can be attributed partly to their being at the right place at the right time. In other words, LUCK! They did have opportunities to advance socially, and when they consolidated their efforts toward one goal, they were successful beyond all measure—Eisenhower in becoming President of the United States, and Salk in discovering a preventive for polio. Each of them also married an outstanding woman.

The Year of the Tiger—November

Persons born in November of a Tiger Year love the outdoors and usually detest desk work. Even if they are file clerks or secretaries, they need some power to decide things, or to be in a position where making decisions is of some importance.

November Tiger Year persons tend to push what they think is right. But by this forcing, they can easily lose all.

Physically, November Tiger Year persons are well proportioned and have attractive physiques. Women of this sign have beautiful ankles and are extremely sexual. They also tend to like their jobs so much that they miss opportunities in marriage. November Tiger Year women should marry before they reach the age of twenty-three. If she waits beyond her twenty-third birthday, there is a tendency for the November Tiger Year woman to make more demands of a future spouse with regard to social prestige and income. Sometimes, they will have affairs with married men who are well heeled and who have children.

Males do good work in any kind of employment that will take them into the fresh air. They are not good white-collar workers.

Females of this sign like to be controlled by strong men and should therefore marry July Tiger Year or January Dragon Year men.

November Tiger Year males do best with a March Sheep or a November Rat Year woman. Any woman born in the Year of the Horse would also be good for men of this sign.

Both men and women should not marry anyone born in the Year of the Snake or the Year of the Monkey.

The Year of the Tiger—December

Persons born in December of a Tiger Year have enormous confidence in themselves and in their abilities. With this confidence, they strive for higher positions and a better home. They will make any personal sacrifice they can in order to get prestige and honor. Sometimes, the December Tiger Year person goes overboard with his self-confidence, causing him to make enemies that are powerful.

December Tiger Year persons are very complimentary and are apt to tell you that they admire an article of your clothing, such as your shirt. They do this to such an extent that you feel you have terrific taste. When a girl has a December Tiger Year boyfriend she will tell others that she likes him because "he pays attention to me!"

Women of this sign are skillful in bringing out confidence in others. Also, December Tiger Year females love to work in outside jobs. Usually, after they have children, they will go back to work.

If the husband of a December Tiger Year woman has his own business, his wife will become his right hand. Sometimes, she will be the real boss of the business, letting her husband look as though he is.

December Tiger Year males are prone to make their wives unhappy. They should marry March Rat or February Sheep Year females.

Women born under this sign have good marriages with a February Rabbit, a March Sheep or a January Monkey Year male.

December Tiger Year persons must be careful in their relationships with those people born in either the Year of the Snake or the Year of the Cock.

THE YEAR OF THE RABBIT

General Traits

Persons born in the Year of the Rabbit are very talented. They are also quite ambitious as well. Rabbit Year persons possess discrimination and usually have exquisite tastes. Somewhat detached, Rabbit Year persons have a tendency to become melancholy. They are conservative and, for the most part, will not blindly rush into something. Their lives tend to be placid, even, and steady.

The Year of the Rabbit—January

Those persons born in the month of January during the Year of the Rabbit are extremely free in their outward actions. Inwardly, however, they tend to be most dependent on others. January Rabbit Year persons have kind hearts and will go out of their way to help others in distress. They have good relationships because of this attitude of offering assistance to those in need.

They are very good in occupations that cater to persons—the hotel business, travel consultation, party arrangers, or the night-club business, for example.

Both men and women born under this sign are able to save money no matter how small their income is. They are most thrifty.

Being that this is considered a "cusp" sign, January Rabbit Year persons may find that they have attributes of the previous sign, the Year of the Tiger, especially December Tiger.

January Rabbit Year males should marry December Dog or August Sheep Year females. They also do well with September Horse Year women.

January Rabbit Year females do best with March Snake or March Tiger men.

Persons of this sign should not marry anyone born in the Year of the Cock.

The Year of the Rabbit—February

Those persons born in the month of February during the Year of the Rabbit are among the most straightforward of any sign. They are able to express themselves directly and say what they think; they never talk in circles.

Persons born under this sign are truly skillful talkers and usually use big gestures when they do speak. Other people are attracted to February Rabbit persons because of their ability to talk and express themselves.

If you are having a party, it is desirable to invite a February

Rabbit Year person, as they will create a most delightful mood.

February Rabbit Year women are most interested in styles, whether it be fashion or interior decoration. They are the most style-conscious of all other signs. The female born under this sign will even adorn herself before retiring to her bed, combing her hair, primping and fussing over herself. When a February Rabbit Year female becomes angered, she will comb her hair for an hour or more. Females born under this sign love to spend money, especially on clothes and jewelry.

February Rabbit Year persons have excellent human relationships with others. They know how to listen, a rare trait.

Careers can be made by February Rabbit Year persons in the field of music. They also make good editors and do well in publishing.

When they marry, February Rabbit Year persons become quite serious in their attitude toward their home life. They do not like to bring their work into the home and desire to create a completely different atmosphere from that of their jobs.

February Rabbit Year females do very well with a September Ox or an April Monkey Year male.

Males born under this sign should marry an August Dragon Year or a December Tiger Year female.

February Rabbit Year persons should not marry anyone born in the Year of the Rat.

One of the foremost American opera singers, Leontyne Price (February 10, 1927), is a February Rabbit Year person. She is said to be a most honest, straightforward woman in her dealings with people. Her ability to express herself is well known and she is certainly style- and fashion-conscious. And one of her best physical attributes is her hair.

The Year of the Rabbit—March

Those persons born in the month of March during the Year of the Rabbit are quite lucky. Most things seem to go well for them. Whatever a March Rabbit Year person sets his mind to do, he will succeed in, with little or no difficulty.

The March Rabbit Year person gets bored easily. He must change his job or hobby more often than others.

The luck surrounding persons born under this sign is evidenced by their habitual ability to find things, such as watches, rings or coins. If a pickpocket is being followed, he will invariably get rid of that which he has stolen by putting it in a March Rabbit's pocket or handbag.

March Rabbit Year females are usually most attractive. They are admired and liked by others. However, it is difficult for them to not get bored and to keep one thing for a long time, whether it is a relationship or a husband. They must work to become more stable than they are.

Both men and women born under this sign have countless opportunities to travel abroad. They must be careful to avoid traffic accidents.

March Rabbit Year females should marry only strong-minded men. A February Boar or February Snake Year male would be ideal for them.

March Rabbit Year males do best with a September Sheep or a June Monkey Year female.

Persons of this sign should be careful of relationships with people born in the Year of the Dragon.

Arturo Toscanini (March 25, 1867) was a March Rabbit Year person. No matter what obstacles he had to contend with, Maestro Toscanini was able to overcome them. He did have many opportunities to travel abroad and is said to have needed changes and challenges in his life.

The Year of the Rabbit—April

Persons born in the month of April during the Year of the Rabbit are decidedly idealistic. Their ideals tend to be too lofty at times, and they will lose out if they don't bring themselves into reality. April Rabbit Year persons always complete their jobs and usually do them well. However, after having finished their jobs, they will wonder if they have done them satisfactorily. This worry often drives them to distraction.

April Rabbit Year persons are loners. They do not like to be bothered by others. Even after marriage, they must have time when they can be completely alone.

Persons born under this sign are very good at design. They could make careers in graphic, industrial, or automobile design. Their jobs should be free-lance work as opposed to employment in one particular office or company.

April Rabbit Year persons tend to be critical and would do well to look for the good points in others, or they will lose out on friendships.

Males born under this sign have a lot of pride. They should find wives who are modest.

Women born in the month of April of a Rabbit Year should marry a January Dog or April Ox Year male.

April Rabbit Year males should marry an April Ox female.

Both men and women of this sign would not do well with anyone born in the Year of the Dragon.

The American writer, Washington Irving (April 3, 1783), was a typical April Rabbit Year person. He was an idealist of the most lofty nature. There were times in his life when he had to be alone, and of course, his writing was of a free-lance nature. Criticism was a most important part of his life's work.

The Year of the Rabbit—May

Those persons born in the month of May during the Year of the Rabbit have a tendency to inherit the characteristics and personalities of their parents, especially the more positive aspects. Usually they inherit money as well.

May Rabbit Year persons desire to help others and do well in social or philanthropic work. They live by the rule "Do unto others as you would have others do unto you." However, they do expect to receive in return.

Persons born under this sign are truly jacks-of-all-trades. They usually hold many kinds of positions. They change their jobs very often as they are able to fit into various employment situations.

May Rabbit Year persons have strong vitality and good health.

In specific occupations, they do very well as managers, especially of distribution and production. Any kind of a trade business is good for them.

Men should marry a September Monkey Year female.

Women do well with an August Cock, October Rabbit, or a March Tiger Year male.

Both male and female May Rabbit Year persons should not marry a person born in the Year of the Rat.

Queen Victoria (May 24, 1819) certainly did inherit her position from her parents, as well as great wealth. She was known for her desire to help others and did live by the "do unto others . . ." rule. You might say that she was in an employment situation that called for management.

The versatility of May Rabbit persons is pointed up by the fact that many dissimilar personalities were born under this sign. Bob Hope (May 29, 1903) and Walt Whitman (May 31, 1819) are both May Rabbit Year persons. They both were interested in helping their fellow human beings and both possessed strong vitality and good health. As evidenced by the vast fortune that he has amassed, Mr. Hope has proven himself to be a far better manager than even a comedian.

The Year of the Rabbit—June

Those persons born in the month of June during the Year of the Rabbit are honest and straightforward. Sometimes, they are unable to express their straightforwardness, as there is a tendency for them to be a bit cowardly. They should learn to overcome this and do as they feel. June Rabbit Year persons will, if need be, sacrifice a lot for the purpose of remaining honest.

Persons born under this sign should not do too many things. They must concentrate all their energies into one particular area, and then they will be most successful. They must make a definite plan for their future if they are to reach the heights of success.

June Rabbit Year females tend to seek opinions on almost every matter before they act. Even if they are purchasing paper cups, for example, they will ask another person if the cups should be blue, yellow, or green. Women of this sign are quite nervous about matters concerning love or sex. They also like to gossip about others and have an uncanny knack of being able to find the bad aspects in any other person's character.

Before making an important decision June Rabbit Year persons should see a qualified person in the matter and not take the opinion of just anyone.

Females of this sign should marry a March Cock or November Rat Year male.

Males would do best with an October Sheep or a July Horse Year woman.

They should not marry anyone born in the Year of the Dragon or the Rat.

The Year of the Rabbit—July

Persons born in the month of July during the Year of the Rabbit appear to be intelligent and stable. However, the July Rabbit Year person tends to worry and become anxious about things. This holds him away from progress, and he must learn to be more bold.

To a great degree, persons born under this sign are lucky. They not only inherit their parents' talents, but their fortunes as well.

July Rabbit persons should specialize. In their middle years, they should remain in their employment situations and not change too often.

In matters of the heart and in friendship they like everybody. A woman born under this sign will date many men, all with different social backgrounds and physical characteristics.

July Rabbit Year persons know their own minds and cannot do anything against their will. If they do not want to do something, it is impossible to force them to do so. In any given situation, they will make a detailed survey before acting. Because of this studious, investigative mind, they tend to be robot-like in their dealings with others, and they actually have to fight with themselves to become more humanized.

Males born under this sign should marry October Boar or June Tiger Year females.

Women born in July of a Rabbit Year should marry a July Rat Year or January Ox Year male.

Both men and women of this sign should not marry a person who was born in the Year of the Cock.

The Year of the Rabbit—August

Persons born in August during the Year of the Rabbit are not at all cowardly, which tends to be a negative attribute of the other months that make up the Year of the Rabbit. August Rabbit Year persons have very strong will and are fighters.

Persons born in August of a Rabbit Year do not have very intelligent outward appearances. Sometimes, their physical looks will prevent them from progressing in employment because of this. They are constantly made to prove the intelligence they do possess.

August Rabbit Year persons will work on something they want to accomplish until they drop from exhaustion. If you take them to the beach, they will build elaborate sand castles, working constantly and continually until they are finished to their satisfaction, even if the sun goes down.

August Rabbit Year persons would rather live in the city than the country. They find an elegant, social mood is most important to their well-being.

Women born under this sign love to attend parties and are the social butterflies of their group. When invited to a social gathering, August Rabbit Year females will attend even if a violent storm is in progress; nothing will stop them, much to the displeasure of their husbands. An August Rabbit Year female tends to be a bit wild.

Women born under this sign should marry an April Rat or December Snake Year male.

August Rabbit Year males do best with a May Ox Year female.

Both males and females of this sign should not marry anyone born in the Year of the Cock.

A most interesting example of an August Rabbit Year person is Fidel Castro (August 13, 1927). Everyone must admit that the man is not cowardly and that he possesses a strong will and is a most able fighter for his cause. His outward appearance is not too intelligent-looking. Fidel Castro has been known to literally drop from exhaustion while he accomplishes that which he wants.

The Year of the Rabbit—September

Those persons born in the month of September during the year of the Rabbit have a most decided dual personality. A part of the September Rabbit Year person is introverted. At other times, the September Rabbit Year person wants and needs to do as he feels, no matter what the outcome.

The dual aspects of this sign carry through on many levels. September Rabbit Year persons, for example, may become involved in a great deal of physical activity, although they possess a most intellectual personality. The reverse of this is also true.

Many artists are born in September of the Year of the Rabbit, and this is a good occupation for these people. They are not suited for organizational employment.

In the field of art, September Rabbit Year persons excel. They also make good technicians and engineering specialists.

Males of this sign do well with a January Tiger, June Boar, or a February Cock Year female.

Women of this sign should marry January Sheep, March Cock, or September Snake Year males. Sometimes, the women of this sign have difficulty finding a suitable spouse and should consider a marriage consultant or even a matchmaker (or computer).

September Rabbit Year persons do not do well with those persons born in either the Year of the Dragon or the Year of the Rat.

The Year of the Rabbit—October

Persons born in the month of October during the Year of the Rabbit are utterly and, almost hopelessly, sentimental. They are attracted to old things and will try to hold onto the past. You will find many antiques in a home that is owned by an October Rabbit Year person.

October Rabbit Year persons are true romantics! They dream of the good times they have had in the past and can forget the bad times. They love nostalgia and anything connected with the past.

Many people who desire the modern things of life will openly criticize the October Rabbit Year person's attraction for the old. But the October Rabbit Year person should not listen to the mutterings of others if he wants to retain his individuality.

You will find that if you have an October Rabbit Year person as a friend, he is apt to have a collection of stamps, matchbook covers, coins, antiques, books, poems or the like.

October Rabbit Year persons make the best antique tradesmen. Because of their romantic nature, they also do well in the field of writing, especially novels and poems.

It is said in the Orient that an October Rabbit Year woman will remain on good terms with her in-laws, even at the expense of her husband. In other words, the in-laws will usually side with a woman born in October of a Rabbit Year rather than with their own son.

The chances are that October Rabbit Year persons will have wonderful marriages if both sets of parents happen to know each other.

Men born under this sign should marry women born in the month of May of a Rabbit Year or March of a Monkey Year.

Females of this sign do best with a March Dog Year male.

Both men and women of this sign do not usually do well with those persons born in the Year of the Cock or the Year of the Rat.

The Year of the Rabbit—November

Persons born in the month of November during the Year of the Rabbit are quite conservative. Other persons admire them for their modesty and their ability to remain quiet. However, they do lose many advantages in society, because they tend to be too conservative. Even if they have questions about something important to them or about their jobs, November Rabbit Year persons will generally try to find the answer themselves. They must learn to involve others in their problems, or they will lose out.

November Rabbit Year persons highly respect their bosses as well as their parents. They also have knowledge of etiquette and use it.

Persons born under this sign have a tendency to feel obligated toward others and are taken advantage of because of this trait. Other people come to depend on November Rabbit persons far more than they should.

Despite their conservatism, November Rabbit Year persons like sports, especially those done in the gymnasium—swimming, jumping the hurdle, for example. They do not like group sports. November Rabbit Year persons keep their bodies in good shape and do lots of exercise.

In choosing a career, the November Rabbit Year person should not be involved in any kind of occupation where teamwork is necessary. Individual work suits his character better.

Women born under this sign should marry an April Snake Year male.

Men born in November of a Rabbit Year do well with an August Dog Year wife.

Both men and women should not marry persons born in either the Year of the Dragon or the Year of the Rat.

Marie Curie (November 7, 1867) was noted for her ability to work alone and for her conservatism as well. Teamwork was not for her, and it was on her own that Madame Curie made her great discovery. Her etiquette was exemplary.

The Year of the Rabbit—December

Those persons born in December during the Year of the Rabbit exemplify the traits of the Rabbit Year to the utmost degree. Their thinking is honest, they speak in a straightforward manner, and they do not take advice too easily. December Rabbit Year persons usually pursue one goal at a time until it is reached.

December Rabbit Year persons have a tendency to appear inhuman. Others around them think that they have neither blood nor tears. It is only in front of lovers or close relatives that their human qualities will be permitted to surface.

Women born in this month and year tend to be a bit sharp-tongued. They like to be evil. For example, if a December Rabbit Year woman observes someone doing something he shouldn't, she will very loudly bring it to the attention of others around that person, causing him much embarrassment. Women born under this sign also love to play practical jokes and make excellent comics.

Careers for persons born under this sign can be made in the fields of politics, journalism, or science.

Men born under this sign should marry a March Cock, December Monkey, or an August Tiger Year female.

Women born in December during a Rabbit Year do well with an October Tiger Year husband.

Both men and women born in December during the Year of the Rabbit should not marry anyone born in the Year of the Dragon.

Frank Sinatra (December 12, 1915) is a most typical December Rabbit Year male. He is frank and straightforward no matter what people think, and he doesn't take advice. Accused of being inhuman on many occasions, he has proven differently time and again when he allows his human qualities to come to the fore. As for politics, Mr. Sinatra may well prove himself in this area at a future time.

THE YEAR
OF THE DRAGON (LIZARD)

General Traits

Persons born during the Year of the Dragon are usually healthy and very energetic. They do possess short tempers and can be quite stubborn. Honesty and courage are other attributes of persons born under this sign. There is a tendency for Dragon Year persons to be worrisome and far too fastidious. In the Orient, the Dragon sign symbolizes life and growth, affording those born during a Dragon Year both longevity and success in their work.

The Year of the Dragon (Lizard)—January

Persons born in the month of January during the Year of the Dragon are perpetual students. Before committing any kind of action, they will first study the situation very carefully. January Dragon Year persons possess much stability and can be quite aggressive.

Being that this month is on the cusp, it would be wise for the January Dragon Year person to look up the previous sign, the Rabbit, especially December Rabbit.

January Dragon Year persons have steady, continous luck in their lives. They do appear to progress more slowly than any other sign, but they accomplish whatever it is they are trying to do little by little, taking one step at a time. Their success in life can be attributed to this steady, slow but ever progressive pace.

Women born under this sign are very female—they love to cook, arrange flowers, and sew. Their thinking is very rational. Sometimes they will argue with their husbands, but within a few hours, all is forgotten. They make exceptional wives.

January Dragon Year males are very tough in business and sometimes hard to deal with. At home, however, they tend to become quite lazy, taking a nap even before retiring.

Women of this sign should marry a November Ox male.

January Dragon Year males do very well with a September Ox or October Dragon Year female.

Both men and women of this sign should be careful in their relationships with those persons born in the Year of the Dog.

The Year of the Dragon (Lizard)—February

Those persons born in the month of February during the Year of the Dragon have a most clearly defined sense of judgment. They also possess strong powers of concentration. If a February Dragon Year person gets an idea, he will almost always make the idea a reality.

February Dragon Year persons are logical and make aggressive leaders!

Both males and females of this sign are gentle, kind, and quite pleasant. Women born in the month of February during the Year of the Dragon have a very intelligent appearance and others will sometimes not approach them because of this, fearing that they may be snobbish. They are usually not snobbish, however.

February Dragon Year females tend to have aspects of their nature that are not immediately apparent to others. Even after several years have passed, friend or mates of February Dragon Year persons will be heard to utter, "I thought that I understood you, but I really don't!"

Males and females of this sign are attracted to slightly muscular, very physical lovers or mates. Anyone who has a February Dragon Year person as a lover will have a most romantic time.

Women born under this sign should marry January Sheep Year males. A man born in the Year of the Rat would also make a fine mate.

February Dragon Year males do best with May Cock Year females.

Both males and females born in February during the Year of the Dragon must be careful of back trouble.

February Dragon Year persons should be careful of those people born in the Year of the Ox or the Year of the Rabbit.

The Year of the Dragon (Lizard)—March

Persons born in the month of March during the Year of the Dragon are most sensitive to their surroundings. If they come upon a lovely landscape or a great work of art, their reaction is more extreme than that of other people. However, March Dragon Year persons have great egos. This combination of sensitivity and ego affords the March Dragon Year person a dual personality. He is able to polish each aspect of his duplicity and use it for his advantage.

March Dragon Year persons usually make their mark in society. When placed in a competitive situation, March Dragon

Year persons never hide the methods they use to gain success. They are most honest with whoever they deal with, and this forthright honesty in competition helps them to get ahead quicker than those with whom they are competing.

March Dragon Year persons have very long professional lives. They are especially talented in the fields of sports or the theater. Many actresses are March Dragon Year women.

Females born under this sign tend to have strong personalities and appear masculine physically. Sometimes, they even wear masculine clothes (pantsuits, slacks or heavy shoes). They are usually not lesbians, but have a difficult time proving this point and fending off homosexual women. In the presence of men, the March Dragon Year female becomes very feminine and will even act motherly. These women should seek out strong, energetic men.

Females of this sign do best with a strong July or September Dog Year male.

Males should marry April Sheep Year women.

Both male and female March Dragon Year people must be careful in their relationships with those persons born in the Year of the Rabbit or their own sign, the Year of the Dragon.

Edward Albee (March 12, 1928) is a typical March Dragon Year male. This contemporary American playwright is most sensitive to his physical surroundings, as evidenced in his plays. His ego is said to be boundless. He had been able to incorporate this duality into his work with tremendous success. He has made his way in society as well.

The Year of the Dragon (Lizard)—April

Those persons born in the month of April during the Year of the Dragon abound with human kindness and understanding. They never pay attention to the small things that seem to bother others around them. Their thinking is always on a big scale. They are also very sensible.

April Dragon Year persons never become disappointed. If they do not get something they want or have worked for, they simply wait for the next opportunity.

Those persons born under this sign usually make big gestures. Often they express happiness or sadness in this fashion. It is easy for them to laugh or to cry. They do not hide their emotions.

Men born in April of a Dragon Year will go out of their way to be friendly to those around them. If they are at a bar, for example, they will befriend the person on the next stool, male or female, and end up paying for the drinks.

Women born under this sign have tremendous energy and vitality. If they sense that a male is their type, they will become very aggressive, sometimes too much so. The lower portion of an April Dragon female's body tends to be large, especially the hip area.

Females born in the month of April in a Dragon Year should marry January Dog or November Cock Year males.

April Dragon Year men do best with April Ox or July Rat Year women.

Both men and women of this sign should not marry anyone born in their own sign, the Dragon.

Both Sir John Gielgud (April 14, 1904) and Yehudi Menuhin (April 22, 1916) are typical April Dragon Year men. They have each been blessed with enormous human understanding and kindness. In their performances they are constantly reaching for a bigger scale. Both of them do utilize gestures as they perform. Friendliness is a trait also attributed to these two wonderful artists.

The Year of the Dragon (Lizard)—May

Those persons born in the month of May during the Year of the Dragon are always cheerful, kind, and very sociable. Usually, everyone likes and admires the personality of a May Dragon Year person. When in company, he wants to be the host.

May Dragon Year persons make fine leaders. They also love beauty and are very sophisticated. Clothes, jewelry, and beautiful things are very important to people born under this sign.

They are almost always pleasant. It is indeed difficult to find fault with the May Dragon Year person. However, if one must find bad points, they have two. First, they possess short tempers. Secondly, they tend to change their minds too often.

Men born under this sign make very good sportsmen and athletes.

Women born in May of a Dragon Year are always working on themselves to become more beautiful. They tend to diet more than others. They are also of the clotheshorse type and will spend vast amounts of time with their hair or their makeup. Usually, the bother pays off, for many other people deeply admire the beauty of a May Dragon female, not realizing that she has created this beauty herself.

May Dragon Year females tend to be more outgoing than males born under this sign. They have what was called in early American history "the pioneer spirit." They will step into danger before their man will. They make excellent detectives, especially in department stores or other public places. With their husbands, however, they become quite childlike and very timid.

Males of this sign should marry April Dog or February Cock Year females.

Women born in May of a Tiger Year would do best with a May Snake Year male.

Both male and female May Dragon Year persons should not marry those persons born in the Year of the Ox.

Both men and women born under this sign should not overwork, as they tire easily.

The Year of the Dragon (Lizard)—June

Persons born in the month of June during the Year of the Dragon have a great deal of pride. They want to have social standing and will spend much money to attain the prestige they desire. They continually spend money to further their social position.

June Dragon Year persons hardly ever borrow money. If they do go out with others who insist on paying the tab, a June

Dragon Year person will say, "Let's make it Dutch then, okay?" When a June Dragon Year person is forced to borrow money, he will do so from one of his good friends, but only on the condition that an interest is paid to that person.

They are not fortunate people and usually have many obstacles to overcome. June Dragon Year persons must work for everything they have in life. Helen Keller (June 27, 1880) was a typical June Dragon Year woman. The obstacles in her path were beyond belief. She possessed pride and a desire for a good social position in life. She certainly had to work for everything she ever accomplished.

Women of this sign are spotlessly clean and also religious. They are romantics as well. Rarely, if ever do they indulge in premarital sexual activity.

June Dragon Year men should marry August Cock Year females.

A woman born under this sign should be with an August Ox Year male if she desires the most happiness.

Both men and women of this sign should not marry a person born in either the Year of the Rabbit or the Year of the Dragon, which is their own sign.

The Year of the Dragon (Lizard)—July

Persons born in the month of July during the Year of the Dragon are predominantly very open in character. They are also quite popular and possess vast energy, which they tend not to conserve.

Males born under this sign have a tendency to be what might be termed a bit feminine. They have a desire to care for others (they make excellent male nurses), and they also worry too much about small matters. Even an athletic type born under this sign, when in the presence of a woman, will not be very masculine. He is liable to adjust his date's collar, pick a hair from her dress, or brush dandruff from her shoulder. He will make sure that she is returned home at an early hour when they date. July Dragon Year men lose out on many opportunities with women because of this. Even in matters of sex, the July Dragon Year male will say such things as, "I really hope that you are not going to hate me afterward!" This, quite naturally, breaks any kind of a romantic mood that might have prevailed.

Males of this sign are quite domestic and will take care of the baby if it cries at night. They sometimes will even do the cooking and laundry. They must be careful to marry women who will understand and appreciate this domestic personality.

Both men and women of this sign use great energy. No matter what kind of work they are involved in during the week, July Dragon Year persons become "Sunday workers"—cleaning the attic, making shelves or bookcases, doing housework or house repairs. They hardly ever rest on their day off. Even during vacation time, they will do work on their homes rather than rest and go away.

Careers can be made by July Dragon Year persons in the field of fashion design. They do well in most areas of art (especially as art critics). Scholastic professions are also good for July Dragon Year persons.

July Dragon Year females are very personable and extremely honest. They do tend to be a bit overcurious and, if not controlled, can easily involve themselves in matters that do not concern them.

Women born under this sign should marry April Dog or October Cock Year males.

July Dragon Year males do very well with February Rat Year females.

Women of this sign should not ever marry a Tiger Year male, especially February Tiger.

The Year of the Dragon (*Lizard*)—*August*

Those persons born in the month of August during the Year of the Dragon are the most creative of their sign. Both in business and in their private life, they utilize the creative aspects of their nature. If an August Dragon Year person lives in a one-room apartment, he will decorate it as though it were a mansion. August Dragon Year persons can purchase a most inexpensive item, and within a short time, they will redo it into something quite stunning.

Both males and females of this sign have many children when they marry. They love children.

Other people tend to come and seek advice from an August Dragon Year female, and with due cause, as she is able to solve many different kinds of problems.

Both males and females of this sign can be successful in whatever kind of job they choose. Rarely do you find them specializing in any particular field.

Females of this sign have extremely developed upper portions of their bodies.

Men born in August during a Dragon Year should marry a March or April Cock Year female.

Females would do best if they married a February Rabbit or October Cock Year male.

Persons born in August of a Dragon Year should not ever marry anyone born in their own sign, the Dragon.

Mae West (August 15, 1892) is a typical August Dragon female. She has many different talents and has been successful in each of them. She is known for assisting friends who come to her with their problems. The upper portion of Miss West's body needs no emphasis here.

The Year of the Dragon (Lizard)—September

Persons born in the month of September during the Year of the Dragon have great confidence in themselves. Their way of thinking is sure and positive, and they rarely if ever make mistakes. Their sense of economics is developed to a very high degree, and they can make out quite well in their investments. They will even lend money to friends, but with a rate of interest.

Men of this sign have a great capacity to concentrate when they are students. They should plan to go into business administration, economics, or related fields. While they are students and early in their business life, they will sacrifice everything for their careers—hobbies, sports, and even dates.

It is said in the Orient that if a girl is afraid of poverty, she should marry a September Dragon Year man, for then she will never have any financial problems.

A September Dragon Year person will sue if he has an accident, for at least six times the real damage costs.

Women born under this sign tend to be realists and are not romantic. Even as children, they have a difficult time understanding the usual adolescent dreams of those their age. The September Dragon Year female is too realistic to chase after romantic rainbows. If one takes a female born in this month to a romantic movie or concert, nine times out of ten she will fall asleep.

September Dragon Year females do very well in the area of crafts, as they can work with their hands. They never spend money needlessly. Their only luxury in life is fine clothing and cosmetics. Usually, they marry at an early age, one to whom they have been attracted as a teen-ager. It is usually not romantic however, as the September Dragon Year woman will one day announce to her family, "I'm going to marry that man!" and this might be the first they even dreamed she was interested in him.

Women born in September during the Year of the Dragon should marry January Tiger or August Sheep Year males.

Men should marry an April Boar, May Rat, or January Ox Year female.

Both men and women of this sign should not marry anyone born in the Year of the Dog.

The Year of the Dragon (Lizard)—October

Persons born in the month of October during the Year of the Dragon have a tendency to act before they think. Because of this quick thinking, they move ahead in a direct line, never straying from the path they are on to reach their goals.

At times, October Dragon Year persons will make mistakes

because of overquick responses. For example: if they are to meet someone for a business luncheon, they will come an hour late, having scanned their appointment book so quickly that the wrong time registered. They will arrive promptly on the hour, but unfortunately, it will be the wrong hour.

October Dragon persons are also honest and brave.

Persons born under this sign are very absentminded. They will place an empty kettle on the stove while preparing coffee or tea. Friends will overlook their absentmindedness because their honesty and good friendship are more important than any quirk of personality the October Dragon Year person may have.

An October Dragon Year male should not be taken too seriously when he professes love to the women in his life. Men of this sign also do not like to be alone and must have others around at all times.

Any woman who marries an October Dragon Year male must be sociable and even learn to attend bars and other forms of night life with him.

October Dragon Year women should marry a January Dragon Year male. Her husband should be at least eight to ten years older than she is.

Males born under this sign do well with November Rat or March Boar Year females.

Both men and women of this sign should be most careful in their relationships with those persons born in either the Year of the Rabbit or the Year of the Ox.

The Year of the Dragon (Lizard)—November

Persons born in the month of November during the Year of the Dragon are the loners of the Dragon sign. They are not aggressive nor even pushy. Even if he is standing first on a line, when others push forward, the November Dragon Year person will allow them to get in front.

November Dragon Year persons have very delicate sense in all matters. They make excellent writers and composers, and should do such work, where they can be left alone. They should never work for large organizations or in a trade, dealing directly with others.

A November Dragon Year woman is a true sophisticate. Usually beautiful, she has knowledge and understanding of all the fine arts—literature, paintings, classical music and ballet. Women of this sign also possess soft, delicate voices. Usually, they dislike sports.

They have inner strength. If her building happens to catch fire, the November Dragon Year woman will go back many times and rescue the things she wants.

Both men and women of this sign should be careful for nervous disorders and mental breakdowns. They are never weak in regard to dealing with their mates and tend to get their own way in most matters.

Men of this sign do well with a March Ox Year female.

Women do well with a December Ox Year male.

Both men and women should not marry anyone born in the Year of the Dog or the Year of the Rabbit.

The Year of the Dragon (Lizard)—December

Persons born in the month of December during the Year of the Dragon have an outward appearance that belies their inner self. They tend to look almost weak but actually possess a strong will. They also have lots of energy, and this, combined with their strong will, usually affords December Dragon Year persons whatever it is they are striving for.

They achieve much social prestige in their life. The nature of a December Dragon Year person is nonaggressive, and he is, therefore, liked by all.

December Dragon Year persons know how to borrow money and how to use it to make more. They are good investors.

Persons born under this sign tend to be absentminded and will sometimes forget what it is they have gone to the store for, bringing back everything but the item needed.

Women born under this sign do not attend to their husbands the way they should. They tend to leave their husbands alone.

When they are young and dating men, however, they tend to ask too many questions of their dates: "Did you enjoy the evening?" "Didn't we have a wonderful time?"

Men born under this sign should marry a November Cock Year female.

Women do very well with an October Ox Year male.

Both men and women of this sign should not marry anyone born in the Year of the Dragon, their own sign.

Woodrow Wilson (December 28, 1856) was a typical December Dragon Year male. His rather weak appearance was in contrast with his inner strong will and energy. He did acquire much social prestige during his life and knew how to use money. He was said to be quite absentminded.

THE YEAR OF THE SNAKE

General Traits

Persons born in the Year of the Snake are usually quite wise. They are also meditative. Snake Year persons tend to be vain and a bit selfish. They are usually quite attractive in their physical appearance. Persons of this sign usually do not have financial problems, and if they do, they overcome them. They are very sympathetic toward others and will try to assist those in need. They overdo almost everything in life.

The Year of the Snake—January

Those persons born in the month of January during the Year of the Snake are noted for their modesty. They do not like anything that is flashy or overdone. Clothes, accessories, and home furnishings of a January Snake Year person reflect his simple, almost somber, manner.

The January Snake Year person is on the cusp of the previous sign, the Dragon, and may have carryover traits of that year, especially December Dragon.

Other people seek out January Snake Year persons for advice on everything from business dealings to personal problems. Wherever they work, or among relatives, the January Snake Year person's judgment and thinking on almost any situation is respected and usually acted upon.

January Snake Year persons make wonderful teachers and professors. They can also have successful careers in psychiatry or as life consultants. Writing is another avenue they could pursue successfully.

January Snake Year persons put a lot of effort in their work and usually, after their thirtieth birthday, they are rewarded with opportunities to advance.

They like to save money but must be careful of gambling, careless investing, and otherwise heedlessly losing their money on poor risks.

Women born under this sign are excellent nurses (especially baby care). They do any work well that concerns children and are good mothers.

The marriages of a January Snake Year person are sometimes arranged by parents or friends. January Snake Year people do not fall in love on sight; it takes them some time before they do love another.

Females of this sign should marry July, September, or December Ox Year persons. The men they marry should be at least five years older than they are.

Males born in January of a Snake Year do best with a February Monkey Year female.

Both males and females should not ever marry anyone born in the Year of the Boar, especially April Boar.

Martin Luther King, Jr. (January 15, 1929) was a typical January Snake Year person. He was modest and conservative in his tastes and manner. The Reverend King's thinking and judgment were certainly relied upon by countless numbers of people. He was a great teacher and did well in writing. After his thirtieth birthday, he began his rise.

The Year of the Snake—February

Those persons born in the month of February during the Year of the Snake are very excitable. They become very involved and emotional and are stimulated quite easily. However, they cool down just as rapidly. If a February Snake Year person likes his job, he will work extremely hard; but his energy capacity is low, and he tires quickly.

If February Snake Year persons can learn to control the excitability of their personality, they will have great success in life before thirty. No matter how poor they might have been, February Snake Year persons get into the upper-middle-class bracket with little effort. Unfortunately, they rarely go beyond this level and hardly ever become rich.

The February Snake Year person has various abilities, such as mastering a foreign language, or making his hobby pay well. Hardly, if ever, does a February Snake Year person need a machine to figure out any kind of calculation. He is able to do large calculations in his head.

February Snake Year persons have marked extrasensory perceptive abilities. They tend to lose this ability when they marry or through some accident.

Men born under this sign are stubborn and do not listen to others, always trying to prove their own way is correct. They are good homebodies, however, and will even seek out a female who reminds them of their mother.

After a February Snake Year female marries, she will want to work and needs this outlet. If they do not become employed after their marriage, February Snake Year females usually immerse themselves in a hobby or become connected with some social work.

A female born in February of a Snake Year should marry a man who can afford her somewhat expensive tastes, such as a January Boar or April Tiger male.

Men born under this sign should marry March Rabbit Year women.

Both men and women of this sign should not marry those persons born in the Year of the Tiger.

The Year of the Snake—March

Persons born in the month of March during the Year of the Snake are most inquisitive. Their suspiciousness does not show on the outside however and tends to be an inward aspect of the March Snake Year person's character.

His investigative nature affords the March Snake Year person opportunities in the fields of detective work, writing, and acting (where detailed work is necessary). His talents are usually recognized early in life, but he rarely acquires much financial reward from whatever it is he goes into.

March Snake Year persons are most honorable, righteous, and just.

Women born under this sign are great lovers of beauty. They constantly dream of beautiful things, physical and spiritual. March Snake Year women will marry for social prestige and fortune, but the man must be handsome as well. They want everything when it comes time for them to marry.

Men of this sign are very suspicious of their women. They tend to think that the women in their life have ulterior motives, and this makes the men reserved. Even after many years of courtship, a March Snake Year male may lose his lover because of this trait.

Women born in the month of March during a Snake Year

should marry August Snake or February Cock Year males.

March Snake Year males do best with an April Sheep Year female.

Men and women of this sign should not marry those persons born in the Year of the Boar.

The Year of the Snake—April

Persons born in the month of April during the Year of the Snake are able to advance in business quicker and more successfully than any other sign! Promotions come easily for them; even in school, they graduate faster than the classmates they started out with. The April Snake Year person will work until he has become the boss, manager, or even vice-president of a company or organization.

Soon after their fortieth birthday, April Snake Year persons are able to have their own business or become executives of the organization they are affiliated with. High society comes easy for them.

The self-confident air of April Snake Year persons is overpowering, and they tend to be disliked for this trait by others. They would rather advance in employment positions than be too deeply involved in friendships.

If the April Snake Year person is to become successful, he should not listen to others but go on his own path, listening to his own inner feelings.

Males of this sign should marry women who are adept at smoothing over the social traits lacking in their husbands; they need this balance.

April Snake Year males do well with an August Ox or a November Rabbit Year female, whose social graces are without par.

Women should marry April Monkey or April Cock Year males. They do well with September Tiger Year males too. If they do marry only for financial gain, they will be most unhappy.

Both men and women should not marry anyone born in the Year of the Tiger.

The Year of the Snake—May

Those persons born in the month of May during the Year of the Snake tend to be nervous and high-strung. They also excite easily. When a May Snake Year person concentrates on one particular thing, he doesn't see, hear, or in any other way sense anything else but that which he is contemplating or doing. A May Snake Year person can suddenly stop whatever it is he is so deeply involved in and leave it forever.

This ability to concentrate with such great power on one thing usually helps the May Snake Year person to advance.

May Snake Year persons are quite passionate in matters of sex. They are versatile in matters of love-making. They are also most devoted lovers and marry only for love, no matter what the social background of their lovers may be.

May Snake Year persons should not drink, as they have a tendency after becoming high to be destructive toward themselves and others. No matter how good their position in life or their profession may be, May Snake Year persons will lose all by the time they reach their thirtieth birthday if they don't curb their short temper and their drinking problems.

Many May Snake Year persons marry more than once. They will, as stated before, marry only for love, but will discover qualities lacking in their mates at a later time, and this will eventually turn them off. In other words, they mature after their first marriage. For this reason, May Snake Year persons should not marry till after the age of thirty. Their second, or sometimes their third marriage is usually good.

Women of this sign should marry April Boar or February Monkey Year males.

Men of this sign do best with a May Dragon Year female. If they marry a second time, a May Tiger Year female would be a good choice.

The Year of the Snake—June

Those persons born in the month of June during the Year of the Snake are quick to judge. Their actions are fast. Cleverness is also an attribute of a June Snake Year person. They tend to have cheerful personalities and are kindly toward others.

Members of the opposite sex are always attracted to June Snake Year persons. But those born in this sign marry either very early in life (sometimes before they leave school) or very late (after the age of forty).

June Snake Year persons have leadership and usually take charge of the group in which they socialize. They are always saying, "Let's get together tomorrow," or "Let's plan a weekend trip together."

The June Snake Year person spends most of the money he makes and has high expenses all through life. Even in business he will spend too much and have to make up the difference with his own money.

Women born under this sign are said to be an "easy mark" for the gigolo type of male. These men will borrow money from the June Snake Year female and not pay it back.

June Snake Year persons are usually attractive, the women being especially well groomed, although a bit flashy in clothes and jewelry.

Persons born under this sign make the best leaders; in organizations, politics, or, in fact, any employment situation. They also demand privacy and have a need to retreat every once in a while. They should have homes or apartments that are away from the hustle and noise.

Men born in June of a Snake Year should marry October Dog or April Horse Year women.

Females born under this sign do very well with an October Snake or an August Dog Year male.

Both men and women of this sign should not marry anyone born in the Year of the Boar.

Frank Lloyd Wright (June 18, 1869) was a typical June

Snake Year male. He was indeed most clever and possessed a cheerful, kindly personality. He took leadership in both his career as the foremost architectural designer of his time and in his private life. Mr. Wright was also known for the periods of his life when he needed complete privacy. He also had a tendency to judge far too quickly.

The Year of the Snake—July

Those persons born in the month of July during the Year of the Snake are most adaptable to any surroundings or changes. They are indeed flexible, able to fit in almost anywhere, in any situation. July Snake Year persons have a tendency to be opinionated. Cleanliness is another attribute of the July Snake Year person.

July Snake Year persons plan their lives and their careers very carefully. Not only do they make plans, but they carry their plans through to fruition.

July Snake Year persons constantly want to change their jobs, but they should not change too often or they will lose out. Their work must be of a creative nature.

July Snake Year persons are not very outgoing and should have work such as composing music or writing, or be in positions where they are important to a company or organization but in a behind-the-scenes capacity.

Women of this sign should not marry domesticated men. Men who like to cook or do housework are not good mates for the July Snake Year female. Men who like business and see their homes only as a place to relax make the best spouses for July Snake Year females.

Also, women of this sign should not take birth-control pills, as they will be unable to conceive when they want to after they stop taking the pill.

Men should marry February Tiger Year females who tend to be modest, shy, and quite conservative.

Females born under this sign do best with October Dog or January Cock Year males.

Jacqueline Kennedy Onassis (July 28, 1929) is a typical July Snake Year female. She has more than proven her ability to fit into any situation and to adjust to any changes. She is said to be quite opinionated and is noted for her clean, fresh appearance. Mrs. Onassis always carries her plans out and likes creative outlets. She is retiring, not too outgoing, despite her position, and did marry two men who were not of the domestic type.

The Year of the Snake—August

Those persons born in the month of August during the Year of the Snake are extroverts. They tend to be flashy dressers, like to drink, and possess a short temper. Despite any shortcomings, however, the August Snake Year person is well liked, as he is most honest.

August Snake Year persons have a keen awareness about things and never take risks. It is quite easy for them to see the pitfalls in any given matter.

Persons born in August of a Snake Year are leaders. Even in school, they become the presidents of clubs or the heads of sports teams.

It is said in the Orient that if an August Snake Year person loves someone in his schooldays, he will have an opportunity to meet that person at a later time and to resume their love. Usually, however, it is just an affair, as they both will not wish to jeopardize their marital position.

Males of this sign are quite handsome. They tend to have happy marriages and constantly work to elevate their wives in regard to education and social graces.

August Snake Year males also have a "dream" female in mind when they are looking for a wife. They usually seek out tall, perfectly proportioned women who have large facial features.

August Snake Year females possess strong characters and for this reason should marry February Rabbit Year males or those men born in May of a Tiger Year.

Males born under this sign do best with April Rat Year females.

Both men and women of this sign should not marry those persons born in the Year of the Monkey.

The Year of the Snake—September

Those persons born in the month of September during the Year of the Snake possess a dominant fighting nature. They do not have a strong will, however. This most unusual combination of a combative spirit plus a weak will brings difficulty into the September Snake Year person's life if he is not careful. He should have friends who are from ten to fifteen years older than himself, persons who can guide and/or control him.

September Snake Year persons have the ability to make money, but if they are not careful, they can lose a great deal of it through poor investing. In stock market matters, they are quite bullish and should learn moderation in this regard.

Females of this sign are noted for their independent, strong personality. They sometimes lose out in romance because of this. September Snake Year females usually have well-proportioned bodies and facial features to match. It is easy for them to become models or motion-picture actresses.

Males born under this sign usually marry understanding women. Both males and females born in September during a Snake Year tend to have intelligent children who have pronounced abilities in many areas but are high-strung and nervous.

Men born in September of a Snake Year should marry September Rabbit Year women. They also do well with March Ox or December Snake Year women.

September Snake Year females should marry December Boar Year men.

Persons of this sign should be most careful in their relationships with people born in the Year of the Monkey or the Year of the Tiger.

Greta Garbo (September 18, 1905) is a typical September Snake Year female. She possesses the physical attributes of a well-proportioned body and face. Greta Garbo most certainly has a fighting spirit and is indeed independent. Her friends were usually quite a few years older than she, including the man who discovered her and brought her to this country.

The Year of the Snake—October

Those persons born in the month of October during the Year of the Snake tend to be quite childlike in appearance and sometimes in manner as well. October Snake Year persons, men especially, do not mature as quickly as others. They have baby faces, and even when they have graduated from college and have worked for several years, a young girl meeting them for the first time will say, "Do you do this work part-time? When do you graduate from school?"

However, many October Snake Year persons have cashed in on their immature attitude and physical appearance by becoming actors and actresses or by becoming involved in a business where the appearance of youth is important—modeling or dealing with teen-agers.

Many outstanding women writers have been born under this sign. October Snake Year women are usually very alert, aware, and keen. They do not chase after material rewards but get them just the same. October Snake Year women can have success in many kinds of businesses, owning their own shop or even company, for example. It is easy for women of this sign to fall in love.

Men born in the month of October during a Snake Year do well in business, but their childlike quality sometimes holds them back. They are not too good in "executive" conversation and lose out there. Those with whom they are doing business have a tendency to feel that the October Snake Year male is not grown-up. In many instances, the October Snake Year male has to wait until after he is thirty years of age for advancement in business or society. He does make an excellent husband and father.

Males born under this sign should marry March Boar or October Horse Year females.

Women would do best with a February Sheep or October Snake Year male.

Both men and women do not do well with anyone born in the Year of the Monkey.

The Year of the Snake—November

Those persons born in the month of November during the Year of the Snake are the most outgoing and cheerful of their sign when they are with other people. When they are alone, however, November Snake Year persons can be quite miserable. They need to have other people around them at all times.

November Snake Year persons have good powers of concentration. They are calm and remain cool in most situations. Because of their enthusiastic nature, many November Snake Year persons have success in life right after they reach the age of thirty.

Females born under this sign mature at an early age. Even when they are seven or eight, the November Snake Year female will show interest in the opposite sex. When they are ten, they will ask boys, "Don't you think I'm pretty?" or "Why don't you like me?" At an early age, they will recognize the fact that their main duty in life is to "catch" a man.

Males of this sign tend to be high-strung, nervous, and a bit envious of others. They are jealous in respect to their lovers or fiancés. Many women in their life cool because of their unfounded jealousy.

When either men or women of this sign marry, it must be for love, or the marriage will not last. They should also have an engagement period of at least one to one and a half years before they do marry.

Women born in November of a Snake Year should marry March Boar men.

November Snake Year males do very well with an October Horse or October Dragon Year female. Women born in the

Year of the Ox are also good mates for November Snake Year males.

Both men and women of this sign should not marry anyone born in the Year of the Monkey or the Year of the Dog.

Grace Kelly (November 12, 1929) is a typical November Snake Year female. She most certainly is outgoing and cheerful when with others and is said to be lonely when not in company. As an actress, she was known for her cool, calm appearance. She did mature at an early age and has admitted a desire to marry into royalty even as a child.

The Year of the Snake—December

Those persons born in the month of December during the Year of the Snake keep on a straight path when they are trying to attain a goal. Once they set their goals, December Snake Year persons will never stray. They express their thinking in a free manner and their character is simple, plain, and direct.

December Snake Year males become jealous of their mates or lovers very easily. They cannot hide this jealousy, which upsets their mates, but in a way, the jealousy proves their deep love.

Other people around the December Snake Year person become distracted by their ability to stay on a direct path to reach any goal. Most people do not have the staying power or the concentration to forge ahead as the December Snake Year person does.

December Snake Year persons make good musicians, as they can practice for countless hours. They do well in any kind of occupation that demands great concentration.

Because of their staying powers, December Snake Year persons have vast success by the time they are thirty-five or thirty-six years of age.

In matters of love, December Snake Year persons are not bashful and can easily express themselves. In fact, they tend to have a problem, as they speak about their love so often that their lover begins to doubt their seriousness.

Women of this sign do best with a September Snake or an April Cock Year male.

December Snake Year males should marry August Rabbit Year females.

Both men and women of this sign should be careful of persons born in the Year of the Boar.

Mao Tse-tung (December 26, 1893) is a December Snake Year male. If it can be said of anyone, Mao Tse-tung has certainly stayed on a direct path in order to reach a goal. His staying power brought great success after his thirty-fifth birthday. His personality is simple and direct.

THE YEAR OF THE HORSE

General Traits

Persons born during the Year of the Horse usually possess cheerful personalities and are well liked by others. They are wise but very impatient. Horse Year persons have a tendency to talk too much. They are very hot-blooded in their relationships with others. Horse Year persons are also independent, more so than the other eleven signs. Rarely do Horse Year persons take advice from others, preferring to act on their own initiative. Horse Year persons are good in money matters.

The Year of the Horse—January

Persons born in the month of January during the Year of the Horse are remarkably clever. If a January Horse Year person fails at anything, he will put extra effort into a second, third, or even a fourth try, and with this fighting spirit, he will go on to win. January Horse Year persons are usually very religious.

Persons born under this sign persist in trying to overcome all obstacles. In their place of employment, they are usually not liked by their boss. However, those over the boss, such as head executive or owner of the business, give them opportunities to move up in position.

The judgment of a January Horse Year person is unequivocally accurate. They do very well in any employment situation dealing with law.

January Horse Year persons are quite systematic; they always make specific plans. They also know their limitations in all things. Overneatness is attributed to the January Horse Year person, as is a strange desire to sometimes make others feel obligated to him.

A January Horse Year person must learn to be strict with himself but also more broad-minded in regard to others.

Men born under this sign should marry a November Boar Year or a September Ox Year female.

January Horse Year women do best with May Boar or April Dragon Year men.

This sign is on the cusp of the Year of the Snake, and certain aspects of that sign, especially December Snake, might be taken into consideration.

Franklin Delano Roosevelt (January 30, 1882) was a January Horse Year person. He was able to overcome countless obstacles, including his physical handicap, to reach his goal of President of the United States. He was very systematic and very clever. His sense of judgment was usually dependable, and he liked law. He was too strict in his demands on others, and in his personal life made others feel obligated to him.

The Year of the Horse—February

Persons born in the month of February during the Year of the Horse are said to be born in one of the most lucky signs. Success, from the time he is young, comes easily to the February Horse Year person. Whenever he starts a project, the February Horse Year person dashes ahead, outdistancing his competition.

Persons born in February of a Horse Year make wonderful sportsmen and athletes. They have a pronounced sense of humor and are the comedians of their group.

Females born under this sign are not very style-conscious; although their clothes are expensive, they tend to be of a conservative nature. If another person compliments the February Horse Year woman on her dress, she knows that the person understands her nature and usually ends up befriending him.

February Horse Year persons are very broad-minded. They do have one failing, and that is that they tend not to understand the backgrounds of those born into less good social positions than they. They will usually try to change that person's standards to meet their own.

February Horse Year persons are honest and sincere. They dislike anyone who lies.

Both men and women of this sign must watch their blood pressure, as it can give them a problem in later years.

Males of this sign should marry July Rat or April Dog Year women.

Women born in February of a Horse Year do best with a February Dog or a September or November Sheep Year male.

Both men and women of this sign should not marry anyone born in the Year of the Ox.

The Year of the Horse—March

Those persons born in the month of March during the Year of the Horse are very demanding of themselves and of others as well. They have countless ideas, and when they learn to focus on one thing, they will have success. The failures in a March Horse Year person's life happen because he expects too much from those around him. This aspect of character must be controlled.

March Horse Year persons are absentminded. When driving a car, their thoughts are completely elsewhere.

Those born under this sign do not like to be asked to do something by others. Once they accept, however, they will finish whatever it is that has been asked of them, no matter how difficult. They can be trusted to complete a job under any circumstances.

March Horse Year persons make good psychologists. They also do well as professional "board-game" players—chess, checkers, etc.

Both men and women tend to lack wit and should marry mates who can make up for this through their own sense of humor.

March Horse Year females are not good housekeepers and should, therefore, seek outside work. They usually have a bad time with their in-laws and under no circumstances should the March Horse Year woman live with her in-laws.

Both men and women of this sign change jobs quite often, even up until their late forties.

Women born in the month of March during a Horse Year should marry December Sheep or July Cock Year men.

Males of this sign do best with a July Monkey Year female. A December Dog Year woman would also make a good wife.

Both men and women of this sign should be careful in their relationships with those persons born in their own sign, the Year of the Horse.

The Year of the Horse—April

Those persons born in the month of April during the Year of the Horse are extroverts. They are also very active, having a high degree of energy. April Horse Year persons love discussions and tend to be very logical.

April Horse Year persons have a tendency to be quite pushy when they want something. They also take advantage of others, but only in small matters. If an April Horse Year male has a girlfriend working at a store, he will ask her if he can use her discount card for any purchases he might make there.

The parents of April Horse Year persons usually get their children into good schools and sometimes even into excellent positions with their influence.

April Horse Year persons are not like bamboo—they do not bend easily with any changes that take place in their lives. If something happens for the worse, it takes April Horse Year persons a much longer time to get over it than other people. They can become seriously depressed and should work to overcome this weakness and to drift with the tide.

April Horse Year persons do have a strong character except when things go wrong, and they should make this aspect of their character even more powerful than it is.

Men born under this sign do best with August Dog Year or November Sheep Year females.

April Horse Year females should marry June Snake, December Monkey, or April Dog Year men.

Both men and women should not marry anyone born in the Year of the Rat.

The Year of the Horse—May

Those persons born in the month of May during the Year of the Horse are usually the brains of an operation. They are wonderful planners but should be in positions where others follow through. It is difficult for them to execute their own plans, no matter how great the plans may be.

Because of their fine planning abilities, May Horse Year persons do well as executives, employers, and politicians.

Although May Horse Year persons have very fine, delicate sense in most matters, they tend to lead lives that are not too well balanced. They must work to attain a balance.

May Horse Year persons change their hobbies quite often.

They will never go back to the same vacation place if they can help it.

May Horse Year persons have a tendency to look like the studious, classical-music-loving type, but usually surprise others by being the opposite.

Men born under this sign are a bit nervous. They should marry a woman older than themselves.

May Horse Year males do best with an April Rat Year woman. A November Rabbit Year female would be a good second choice.

Women born under this sign should marry March Rat or May Monkey Year males.

May Horse Year persons should not marry anyone born in their own sign.

The Year of the Horse—June

Those persons born in the month of June during the Year of the Horse were born to be in the spotlight. Whatever profession they go into, they always end up in front, on display. This is one of the best signs for careers in show business. Their sophisticated style is a great asset in helping the June Horse Year person attain success.

June Horse Year persons spend a great deal of money, and sometimes this gets them into difficulty. It is hard for them to pass something by if they like it, even if funds are low.

Careers are easily made by June Horse Year persons in art, advertising, and the theater.

The June Horse Year person tends to have a great deal of sex appeal. He usually has a well-built body and attractive facial features. A great deal of this sex appeal is generated from within the June Horse Year person, rather than from physical characteristics.

Men born under this sign should marry January Sheep Year females. February Dog Year females are good second choices.

June Horse Year women do best with either March Monkey

Year or July Sheep Year males. Their husbands should be at least ten years older than they are.

The Duke of Windsor (June 23, 1894) is a typical June Horse Year person. He has certainly been in the spotlight all his life and is noted for his sophisticated style in manner and dress. He has spent a great deal of money in his life.

The Year of the Horse—July

Those persons born in the month of July during the Year of the Horse usually have kind, gentle personalities. Their hearts are large, and they are constantly giving of them. It is most difficult for a July Horse Year person to decide anything without consulting others. July Horse Year persons will never act before they consult their mates or families.

July Horse Year males extend their generosity to their employment and are usually rewarded for the extra effort and assistance they freely give. When a July Horse Year male stays overtime, of his own choice, at his place of work, he is repaid a hundred times over by his superiors.

Women born in the month of July during a Horse Year are well liked by everyone. Even their in-laws tend to like them more than their own sons! Also, July Horse Year women usually marry early in life, sometimes when they are still in school. They marry well and in many instances will have opportunities to live in other countries because of their husband's jobs.

July Horse Year persons do very well at table sports (Ping-Pong, etc.). They also are gamblers and make very good card players.

Women born in July of a Horse Year should marry June Rabbit or October Horse Year men.

Males of this sign do best with April Rabbit or November Horse Year women. They should marry women who come from another town rather than their own.

Persons of this sign should not marry anyone born in the Year of the Ox.

The Year of the Horse—August

Those persons born in the month of August during the Year of the Horse are most sensitive. They also judge character well. August Horse Year persons do a great deal of traveling in their life, which they love.

August Horse Year persons will usually act on their first impression. They are most intuitive.

If an August Horse Year person chooses to study in some specific field, he will be a success by the time he is twenty-six or twenty-seven. He is very good in business and usually makes greater strides in his career than those who had started out with him.

If an August Horse Year person feels that he is going to fail at something, chances are he will not attempt to do it. Persons born under this sign hardly ever take chances.

August Horse Year persons have beautiful movements and make fine dancers. They also love music and do well in careers relating to either dancing or music.

August Horse Year persons like to collect mementos of their extensive traveling. They will collect anything—postcards, slides, stones—if these things in some way relate to their travels.

Women born under this sign should marry December Dog Year males. October Sheep Year men are also compatible signs for them.

Males born in August of a Horse Year do well with November Dog Year women.

August Horse Year persons should not marry those people born in the Year of the Rat or the Year of the Horse, their own sign.

Leonard Bernstein (August 25, 1918) is a typical August Horse Year person. He is a most sensitive man and is said to act on his first impressions. Success came at an early age after study in a specific area. When he conducts, his movements are quite beautiful and his career in music is world renowned. Mr. Bernstein has also done extensive traveling in his life.

The Year of the Horse—September

Those persons born in the month of September during the Year of the Horse are simple, direct, and honest. If their friends get into difficult situations, September Horse persons will help them out. However, they will sometimes get into trouble themselves because of this. It is hard for a September Horse Year person to save money.

September Horse Year persons are taken advantage of by others, who regard their simplicity as an opportunity to benefit themselves.

September Horse Year persons fall in love quite easily and are romantics. The lovers of September Horse Year persons will also take advantage of their simple nature.

September Horse Year persons are collectors of many things. Some of their friends are turned off, because they tend to be a bit fanatical when it comes to their collections.

Persons born under this sign are steady and quite reliable. They make wonderful friends.

Men born in September of a Horse Year do best with December Cock or October Rat Year women.

September Horse Year ladies should marry January Rabbit Year men. A male born in the month of March during a Monkey Year is also a good choice.

They should not marry anyone born in the Year of the Ox or of their own sign, the Horse.

The Year of the Horse—October

Those persons born in the month of October during the Year of the Horse are quite kind, most human, and very delightful. They tend to be a bit lazy. October Horse Year persons are noted for their ability to complete jobs started by others. They are able to utilize others' ideas when they produce or create something.

October Horse Year persons are not good in their own business. They should have a boss. The best assistants are October Horse Year people.

Hobbies are very important in the lives of October Horse Year persons. They do tend to go overboard with their hobbies until they are the only thing they think and talk about.

October Horse Year persons are extremely clean. Even as children, they keep themselves neat and clean.

Men born under this sign do very well with March Sheep or December Sheep Year females. In fact, they do well with women born in any month during the Year of the Sheep.

Women born in October during a Horse Year should marry June Ox or October Snake Year males. A November Snake Year male is also compatible for this sign.

Both men and women of this sign would do well to seek out mates who possess education and a high intellectual level. They should not ever marry anyone born in the Year of the Rat.

The Year of the Horse—November

Those persons born in the month of November during the Year of the Horse are the most content people of their sign. They tend to be satisfied with their condition in life, no matter what it is. They are kindly and fun-loving. They also possess the attribute of cleanliness.

November Horse Year persons have orphanlike qualities, as they leave home at an early age and will move to where they do not know anyone. Sometimes they marry persons from faraway lands.

When persons of this sign marry, they depend on each other a great deal, creating a wonderful basis for a good family foundation.

Their satisfaction with conditions prevents them from advancing in business easily. If they go into partnership, they must choose an open and active person. They tend to be a bit lazy, a byproduct of their self-contentment.

Men of this sign do very well with February Horse Year mates. February Tiger Year persons are also compatible.

November Horse Year females should marry September Cock, May Dog, or March Sheep Year males. An April Dog or July Horse Year man would also be a good choice.

November Horse Year persons should not marry anyone born in the Year of the Rat.

Billy Graham (November 7, 1918) is a typical November Horse Year male. He is kind and most human. Neatness and cleanliness are other attributes of the Reverend Graham. He is said to possess a delightful sense of humor.

The Year of the Horse—December

Those persons born in the month of December during the Year of the Horse are broad-minded and kind. They have two definite sides to their personalities. They like to work and they like to play.

It is difficult for December Horse Year persons to get stability into their lives, as they desire constant change—change of job, change of home and activities. They are well balanced, however, despite this need to bring about new conditions.

December Horse Year persons must work on their powers of concentration which are not developed. When they are involved in something, their minds tend to be elsewhere. Quite often, December Horse Year persons are transferred in employment situations, which may be a result of their inner desires.

December Horse Year persons are good writers. They do very well in jobs that involve travel and change of location (salesmen, airline work, etc.).

Women of this month like sports clothes (sweaters, pantsuits, and sometimes very mannish apparel). They like to have a great variety of clothes.

To escape from any humdrum life they might become involved in, December Horse Year males sometimes become barflies.

Men born in this month do well with a September Dog Year

female. A February Rat Year or January Cock Year female would also be compatible signs.

December Horse Year females should marry either August Boar or September Monkey Year men. Anyone born in a Boar Year is compatible for the December Horse Year sign; persons in this sign should not marry anyone born in the Year of the Rabbit.

James Thurber (December 8, 1894) was a typical December Horse Year male. He was kindly and most broad-minded. Change played a most important part in his daily activities. He did become involved in the creative outlet attributed to persons born under this sign—writing.

THE YEAR OF THE SHEEP

General Traits

Persons born in the Year of the Sheep are extremely gentle and are usually quite intelligent. They tend to be overtimid and are sometimes too pessimistic. Sheep Year persons are quite artistic and can make careers in the arts. The manner of a Sheep Year person is dignified. Those born under this sign demand elegance in their lives. Unless they get a direction early in life, Sheep Year persons suffer from pangs of uncertainty. Throughout their lives, however, Sheep Year persons usually have enough of the necessities to free them from want.

The Year of the Sheep—January

Those persons born in the month of January during the Year of the Sheep are most cheerful and remarkably active. They are also very independent. January Sheep Year persons are on the cusp of the preceding sign, the Horse, and might have characteristics of that sign, especially December Horse.

January Sheep Year persons tend to be conservative, too much so. They have a fear of failure and will never take a gamble. They have many opportunities in life, but pass them by because of fear of failing.

Persons born under this sign are plan makers. They will plan everything in their life, from their employment situations to exactly how many children they will have. The plans are always carried out, slowly, one step at a time.

January Sheep Year persons like entertainment and spend much money on this aspect of their activities.

Men of this sign are romantics and work to make that kind of mood whenever in the presence of women.

January Sheep Year females are very good conversationalists and have knowledge of many different kinds of topics. They do not like to date someone unless they feel a marriage will come of it.

Both men and women born in the month of January during a Sheep Year must work on forcing themselves to take gambles, or else they will lose out on countless chances.

Women of this sign do best with a March or an April Snake Year male.

The most compatible signs for January Sheep Year males are August and September Rabbit Year women or February Dragon Year women.

Persons born in January during a Sheep Year must be careful of eye, ear, and throat trouble.

The Year of the Sheep—February

Those persons born in the month of February during the Year of the Sheep are very warm, friendly people. They are the most well liked of their sign. February Sheep Year persons are mild in manner.

If a February Sheep Year person has a failure in life, he is able to forget it almost immediately and go on. He never gives up.

Because they tend to be dreamers and romantics, February Sheep Year persons make wonderful artists, musicians, and designers. They are able to extend their natural, raw talents into professions.

There is a tendency for laziness in persons born under this sign, and they need to put much effort into their dreams if they want them to come to fruition.

If they work for companies or organizations, February Sheep Year persons are usually well liked by those in positions higher than they are. Because of this, they are treated well and are given opportunities to advance in their work.

Women of this sign are very feminine and tend to be thin. They move well and make fine dancers. They can, however, be quite tough. They make the most loyal wives and will never leave their husbands no matter what the situation.

February Sheep Year men tend to be frail and nonmuscular. Sometimes, women are attracted to this almost anemic type.

Women of this sign do well with either November or December Tiger men.

February Sheep Year males are most compatible with women born in any month of the Year of the Tiger, but especially with June Tiger Year women. They also do well with January Dog Year females.

The Year of the Sheep—March

Those persons born in the month of March during the Year of the Sheep are said to have a lucky star over them. They succeed in life quite early and with comparative ease. The March Sheep Year person usually associates with the right people, who sometimes discover and put to use the various hidden talents of this sign. The March Sheep Year person does need someone to act as a catalyst to propel him forward.

March Sheep Year persons are very logical. They are also able to control their emotions, using their logic instead of becoming upset or angry over a situation.

Persons born under this sign have a tendency to look older than they truly are. Sometimes, March Sheep Year persons are introverts. They are not particularly pleasure-seeking and rarely date.

Men of this sign are hard workers. They do not talk very much and are very honest. Employers usually get along with men of this sign exceptionally well. They are trusted in all matters.

March Sheep Year women make the best housewives. They are also sociable. For these two reasons, March Sheep Year women are ideal wives. They do tend to be a bit promiscuous, however, and therefore need a strong man as a husband.

Women born under this sign should marry October Horse Year or November Tiger Year men.

March Sheep Year men do best with a November Horse or a December Horse Year woman.

Persons of this sign should not marry those born in the Year of the Dog or the Year of the Rat.

The Year of the Sheep—April

Those persons born in the month of April during the Year of the Sheep are the loners of their sign. They must have time when they can get completely away from everyone. They do not like to be disturbed by others.

April Sheep Year persons are very good at intricate detail work. They make excellent editors, in all fields, for they are able to spot mistakes quite easily. Other avenues of employment that are advantageous for April Sheep Year persons would be in science and mathematics. They also make the best schoolteachers.

April Sheep Year persons are not very flexible; they tend to be too stiff in most matters and must learn flexibility. The only time they do relax is by drinking or with other physical stimulants. They will then talk a lot when "under the influence." Afterward, they recall nothing.

April Sheep Year persons have classical tastes; they love the ballet, opera, Shakespeare, and great literature.

Persons born under this sign embarrass quickly and never like any kind of empty show. A child of this sign will even tell his parents how to act so as not to embarrass him. He will tell his friends, as he grows older, what kind of clothes to wear if they are to be seen with him. You might hear an April Sheep Year woman say to a friend she is going to meet, "Please, don't wear that red dress that you had on last time; it's a bit too loud."

April Sheep Year persons do not like anything that is not spotlessly clean. For this reason, they are not charitable to those looking for handouts in the street. They will walk away from these situations.

Women of this sign are very timid and shy when dating. However, when they marry, there is usually a reversal, and they tend to become quite bold and outspoken toward their husbands.

Men of this sign do best with women born in either May or June during the Year of the Cock.

Women should marry March Snake Year males. They also do well with men born in any month during the Year of the Rabbit.

Persons born in April during the Year of the Sheep should not marry those born in the Year of the Dog.

The Year of the Sheep—May

Those persons born in the month of May during the Year of the Sheep are most noble in appearance, especially women of this sign. May Sheep Year persons love nature in all its aspects. They should work in occupations where contact with nature is direct—farmer, florist, zoo keeper, or rancher.

Women of this sign are most desirable. They are usually either beautiful or dainty, and they have perfectly proportioned bodies. Their spotless, white skin is another attribute. Truly, more than any other sign, May Sheep Year women are "the ideal females."

Men of this sign are very handsome, although they are usually short. There is a tendency for these men to be "cute" in thinking, actions, and speaking. Older women are attracted to this boyish nature. Sometimes, the May Sheep Year male will play his part to the hilt.

Persons born under this sign are usually asked to parties because of their fine attributes. They also have a mysterious or hidden part of their personality that no one sees, not even husbands or wives. They do not let everything about themselves become known.

If May Sheep Year persons have jobs that are with companies or organizations, the work should be of a creative nature. They make excellent writers and usually can sing well.

Women of this sign should marry June or July Monkey Year males.

May Sheep Year men do best with a woman who is born in any month of the Dog Year, but especially May Dog Year females.

May Sheep Year persons should not marry those people born in the Year of the Rat or the Year of the Ox.

Margot Fonteyn (May 18, 1919), the great ballerina, is a typical May Sheep Year female. She has a most noble appearance. Her physical attributes are perfect—well-proportioned body, beautiful white skin, and lovely face. Part of her success is the fact that one is aware of a mysterious quality when she dances. Margot Fonteyn is said to love nature.

The Year of the Sheep—June

Persons born in the month of June during the Year of the Sheep are said to be most fortunate. They possess extreme good luck. It is easy for a June Sheep Year person to win lotteries or big prizes in contests. If he becomes involved in a lawsuit through an accident, he will become rich.

Money is usually willed to a June Sheep Year person, or

else he marries into money. However, this good fortune could do the June Sheep Year person harm if he does not learn how to control it; the money may rule his life.

June Sheep Year persons are quite cheerful. They also possess a youthlike personality as well as a youthful appearance. They are usually mistaken for five or ten years younger than they are.

June Sheep Year persons give very good first impressions to others. They like people and in turn are liked themselves.

They should choose occupations that involve others. Philanthropy comes easy for the June Sheep Year person. He is also good in social work, dealing in real estate. Many diplomats are June Sheep Year persons.

Women born under this sign are dainty in appearance, small and slim. They tend to like sports clothes. They do well as receptionists, store executives, and in positions that deal directly with others. They usually marry someone they met at their place of business.

Women of this sign do well with a man born in any month of an Ox Year, but especially a July Ox Year male. They also do well with October Boar Year men.

June Sheep Year men should marry a September Rat Year female.

Both men and women should keep away from anyone born in the Year of the Dog.

The Year of the Sheep—July

Those persons born in the month of July during the Year of the Sheep have great tenacity. They hang on until they succeed at something. July Sheep Year persons never walk away from a projected achievement. They have great pride in their work and will not rest until they themselves are satisfied with it, regardless of what others around them feel.

July Sheep Year persons are studious and place great effort into any undertaking. They do tend to be too self-critical.

Persons born under this sign desire stability above all other things. They do not like to change jobs or move around very much. Home is most important to these persons.

July Sheep Year persons are the idealists and romantics of their sign. They are also most patriotic and have a deep, honest love of country.

July Sheep Year persons like to care for others and usually have the means to do so. However, if a July Sheep Year person feels that he is being taken advantage of, he will cut the friendship off immediately.

The July Sheep Year person loves his children. Women of this sign are excellent wives and mothers. They are also most loyal to their husbands.

Both men and women should be careful of stomach and liver problems.

Women of this sign should marry June Rabbit Year men. They also do well with anyone born in the Year of the Boar or the Rat.

Men born in the month of July during the Year of the Sheep do best with Horse Year women, especially June Horse Year females.

Persons of this sign should not marry those born in the Year of the Ox.

The great American lyricist Oscar Hammerstein II (July 12, 1895) was a most typical July Sheep Year person. Against countless odds, he rose in his field. Never once did he let any of his work be published or performed until he was 100 percent satisfied with it himself, regardless of what his partners or representatives thought. Mr. Hammerstein was romantic and idealistic, as evidenced by his lyrics. He did have a philanthropic outlook and did much for others. His love of home is well known, as was his love of children.

The Year of the Sheep—August

Those persons born in the month of August during the Year of the Sheep are the most logical of their sign. They also have a wondrous sense of beauty and can find beauty in most things.

August Sheep Year persons know how to dress, and even in inexpensive, store-bought clothes, they look better than those wearing custom-made, expensive garments.

August Sheep Year persons are usually conservative in all matters. Women born under this sign do not overspend. They never waste one dollar!

Persons born under this sign can be a bit moody. Their approach to all things in life is mild and easy. They like a city atmosphere rather than a country one.

Usually, persons born in the month of August during the Year of the Sheep have good bank accounts or investments owing to their conservative methods of living.

Men born under this sign do very well in jobs concerning women—cosmetics, jewelry, beauty shops, or designing women's fashions.

Women of this sign tend to be a bit masochistic and should learn to overcome this trait.

Women born in the month of August during the Year of the Sheep do very well with those males born in the Year of the Rat, especially September, and also do well with January Rabbit or July Monkey Year males.

August Sheep Year males should marry August or September Dragon Year females.

Both men and women should be careful of those persons born in the Year of the Ox or the Year of the Dog.

The Year of the Sheep—September

Persons born in the month of September during the Year of the Sheep are the most capable of their sign. They are also sincere and dedicated. September Sheep Year persons have one characteristic that must be controlled, and that is that they want to do everything by themselves. This being impossible, they will sometimes fail at something they are undertaking when they don't get outside assistance.

September Sheep Year persons tend to exhaust their energies

too much, trying to prove that they alone can accomplish something. In many cases, bad results will follow from this attitude.

It is difficult for a September Sheep Year person to forget small failures, and he gets a number of nervous disorders if this is not controlled.

Women of this sign are usually of the "cute" type, rather than beautiful. Men are attracted to them physically and also because they are very good listeners. They also let a man believe he is "superior."

Both men and women should be careful of blood pressure and various other blood disorders.

Women of this sign do well with either a February Ox Year male or anyone born under the sign of the Rat.

Men should marry February Horse or September Dog Year women.

Both men and women born in September during the Year of the Sheep should be careful of those born in the Year of the Dog, except for the September Dog.

The Year of the Sheep—October

Those persons born in the month of October during the Year of the Sheep are most realistic in their approach to life. They are also cool in manner and possess quite a bit of intelligence. They will do anything for success in life and business, sometimes at the expense of their families.

October Sheep Year persons (especially males) are good at seeing and understanding financial matters. They usually make the right move in these areas. Outwardly, October Sheep Year males seem concerned about those they come into contact with; inwardly, however, they rarely think about others. They make the "best" politicians and lawyers for this reason.

Occupations for October Sheep Year persons can be made in politics and journalism. They make good editors.

Women of this sign tend to be hypochondriacal, with themselves and with their families. They let their children take the day off from school at the slightest sniffle. They forbid their husbands to work overtime.

Women of this sign make good leaders in all fields and could go far with this ability.

Men of this sign would do best with Horse Year women, especially August Horse. They also do well with March Dog Year women.

Women should marry September or October Tiger or June Rabbit Year males.

Both men and women of this sign should not marry those born in the Year of the Cock or the Year of the Ox.

The Year of the Sheep—November

Those persons born in the month of November during the Year of the Sheep possess very sharp judgment. They are also skillful in the areas of speech. For this reason, many November Sheep Year people are interested in law or government.

November Sheep Year persons are quick, and they complete anything they start. They do tend to be too emotional and changeable. The only thing that may prevent November Sheep Year persons from reaching their goals would be the fact that they cannot make up their minds over small matters.

There is an erratic quality about the November Sheep Year person. He is impulsive in areas where there should be more control. Suddenly, for no apparent reason, a November Sheep Year person will leave a group of friends and run down the street, singing or shouting. Or he will put salt in his morning coffee. A November Sheep Year man (although not homosexual) might dress up in women's clothes and even go out into the street with them on. It is difficult for the November Sheep Year person to control those impulsive thoughts everyone gets; he acts upon them. Usually, he is so well liked by his friends that they tend to overlook the strange things he does.

November Sheep Year persons should not work for staid organizations, such as banks.

Women of this sign are very popular because of their outgoing, happy, giving qualities. They do have a tendency to talk too much.

Men born in the month of November during the Year of the Sheep should marry April Tiger Year females. Also, anyone born in the Year of the Dog, in any month, would be a good match.

Females of this sign do best with April Horse or July Boar Year men. Those males born in the Year of the Sheep are also acceptable.

Both men and women should not marry anyone born in the Year of the Rat or Rabbit.

The Year of the Sheep—December

Those persons born in the month of December during the Year of the Sheep are the most kindly of their sign. They always try to help others, even at the cost of being hurt themselves. December Sheep Year persons do go overboard on this aspect and tend to be Don Quixote types, too idealistic.

December Sheep Year persons have great romantic and idealistic dreams. Usually they fail at these dreams when they try to put them into action. When this happens, they blame the world for the failures, becoming quite depressed.

December Sheep Year women can be easily taken advantage of. They must be careful of men who promise them marriage, get what they want, including the December Sheep Year female's savings, and then disappear. There is a saying in the East that you can smooth-talk a December Sheep Year woman out of anything!

It usually isn't until well after his thirty-fifth birthday that the December Sheep Year person matures and becomes realistic. He usually has difficult times until his thirtieth birthday.

Men born under this sign do best with women born in the Year of the Horse, especially March and April Horse Year females. They also do well with December Monkey or April Cock Year women.

Women born in the month of December during the Year of

the Sheep should marry persons born in the Year of the Boar. An October Horse Year male would also make a good spouse.

Both men and women of this sign should be careful of those persons born in the Year of the Dog or the Year of the Ox.

THE YEAR OF THE MONKEY

General Traits

Persons born in the Year of the Monkey are intelligent, clever, and very skillful. It is easy for Monkey Year people to become discouraged, even though they are inventive and original in both their way of thinking and carrying out their plans. Persons born in the Year of the Monkey possess abundant common sense. Monkey Year persons tend to be sexual. However, they can become cool and dispassionate when they so choose. Persons born under this sign make good leaders and do well in large-scale operations.

The Year of the Monkey—January

Those persons born in the month of January during the Year of the Monkey have a mild manner. They never show off and are not critical of others. Being that this is a cusp sign, it might behoove the January Monkey Year person to read up on the traits of the previous sign, the Year of the Sheep, especially December Sheep.

January Monkey Year persons are very active, as they usually have great energy.

January Monkey Year persons do not intrude upon or in any way bother other people, and they in turn do not like to be bothered.

Persons born under this sign work very well with their hands, especially in arts and crafts. They also make good architectural engineers, or designers.

There is a tendency for the January Monkey Year person to be a bit selfish. Even if he has wonderful ideas for the business he is in, he will not offer these ideas unless it means that he will advance in some way.

January Monkey Year persons tend to have blood-pressure problems that affect their metabolism. They are usually not alert by day but wake fully by evening. They are the night people of their sign.

Men born under this sign should marry December Tiger Year women. Persons born in any month of the Year of the Boar would also be good mates.

Women born in January of a Monkey Year do best with a January or February Rabbit Year male or any Rat Year male. Men born in the Year of the Sheep also make excellent spouses for January Monkey Year women.

Both men and women should be careful of any person born in the Year of the Snake.

The Year of the Monkey—February

Those persons born in the month of February during the Year of the Monkey are extremely kind and cheerful. They are very popular with the opposite sex and are well liked. February Monkey Year persons are the comics of their sign.

February Monkey Year persons make good leaders and managers. In business, they usually become executives. They are good at club activities, both when they are in school and later on.

The February Monkey Year person can forget the bad things that happen in his life.

Persons born under this sign love to gather groups of friends and become their leader in club activities, or travel situations.

February Monkey Year persons have a secretive side to their personality. They do not tell all about themselves, even to their families or close friends. They like to be around others despite their secretive nature and become quite depressed when left alone for some time.

Persons born under this sign do not look like executive types, and because of their appearance, they are sometimes held back from advancing in employment situations.

Men of this sign do best with March and April Tiger Year females and May Snake Year women as well.

Women born in February of a Monkey Year should marry January Snake Year or any month of the Rat Year males.

Both men and women should not marry anyone born in the Year of the Boar.

The Year of the Monkey—March

Persons born in the month of March during the Year of the Monkey are said to be the most immaculately clean of all the signs. They demand cleanliness in every situation, not only physical cleanliness, but mental wholesomeness as well.

They are very good workers. Even though they usually have no great desire to be promoted, their bosses give them large promotions, because of the fine, steady work they accomplish.

They are most conservative in manner but are always asked to head clubs (such as PTA or bridge clubs).

Both men and women of this sign love beauty and must have

beautiful things around them. They are also usually the best dressers of their sign. Constantly aware of their appearance, they buy only the best clothes and accessories.

Once a March Monkey Year person begins a job, he will not rest until it has been completed perfectly, even if he doesn't like what he is doing.

There is a tendency for March Monkey Year people to become involved with married persons, especially after they pass the age of thirty. They must be careful of this; it is opposed to their nature and could prove to be destructive.

Women born under this sign do best with males born in the Year of the Rat, especially December Rat. October and November Rabbit Year males are also good for them.

Men born in the month of March during the Year of the Monkey do well with December Sheep, September Horse, or June Rat Year females.

Persons of this sign should not marry anyone born in the Year of the Snake or the Year of the Boar.

The Year of the Monkey—April

Those persons born in the month of April during the Year of the Monkey are energetic. Because of their excessive energy, April Monkey Year persons make progress in their daily life. They do very well in money matters and hardly ever lack money.

April Monkey Year persons have countless friends, although they usually do not have one specific one to depend on. When he is in the company of his friends, the April Monkey Year person can feel lonely and a bit introverted.

Women of this sign make the best nurses, as they like to care for others. They make good assistants for their husbands and are excellent wives. They are hard workers and always put their husbands and children before themselves.

Men of this sign are adroit in financial matters. They should be in business situations where they can capitalize on their originality and inventiveness.

Women born in the month of April during the Year of the Monkey do best with husbands that are born in the month of

May during the Year of the Rabbit, or men born in either July or August of a Boar Year. Too, they do well with October Rat Year males.

Men should marry February Rabbit or April Ox Year females.

Both males and females of this sign should be careful of those people born in the Year of the Tiger.

Physically, the lung area of an April Monkey Year person is the weakest part and should be watched.

The Year of the Monkey—May

Persons born in the month of May during the Year of the Monkey possess sharp, alert minds. They also know their limitations in all things. Sometimes, this works to their disadvantage, as they tend to never take a chance.

There is a saying in the East that a May Monkey Year person is too smart for his own good. If he is born with talent, he usually feels that that is enough and does not learn how to hone his abilities.

May Monkey Year persons can be quite nervous, which stems from the fact that their work is not more recognized. Great stress is usually placed upon a May Monkey Year person.

May Monkey Year persons do well in all phases of journalism, photography, designing, and publishing. They usually have success in business owing to their good sense.

In their early years, May Monkey Year persons lose either their lover or closest friend, usually over a misunderstanding. They never forget this loss, and it usually is the main factor in their maturing.

There is a tendency for the May Monkey Year person to us alcohol and drugs as a tranquilizer. If he chose to relax with light sports (tennis, swimming, etc.), he would be much better off.

May Monkey Year persons possess fine memories and can remember small details. They do a lot of reading and retain all that they read.

Men born under this sign do well with women born in any

month during the Year of the Horse, but especially May Horse.

Women born in May of a Monkey Year should marry September or October Snake Year men or any Rat Year male.

Both men and women must be careful of anyone born in the Year of the Boar.

Bertrand Russell (May 18, 1872) was a May Monkey Year person. Possessor of a keen, alert mind, Mr. Russell did do a great amont of writing. He had a fine memory and was said to have a tendency toward nervousness.

The Year of the Monkey—June

Persons born in the month of June during the Year of the Monkey are said to possess a Latin spirit. They become excited very easily and cool off just as fast. June Monkey Year persons are moody; they cry for little or no reason. The life of a June Monkey Year person can be quite frantic.

June Monkey Year persons become quite lonesome when they are left alone. It is difficult for them to exist without others around them.

Persons of this sign are easily stimulated, physically and mentally. They must learn to control this overstimulation, or it will lead them to great difficulty in life.

Music is very important in the life of a June Monkey Year person. Usually, he has a beautiful voice.

Persons born under this sign tend to agree with others a bit too much. They are more comfortable agreeing with others, even if they feel different inwardly.

Men of this sign are usually very thin and have long arms and legs.

Women born in June of a Monkey Year do well with men who were born in either October of an Ox Year or March of a Rabbit Year or any Rat Year male.

Men of this sign do best with May Sheep Year females. Women born in the Year of the Rabbit, especially in March and April, also make good spouses for them.

Both men and women must be careful of anyone born in the Year of the Tiger.

The Year of the Monkey—July

Persons born in the month of July during the Year of the Monkey are the jack-of-all-trades of their sign. They are skillful in all fields and trades. The July Monkey Year person is most adaptable, and even when moved around in his organization or place of business, he accepts the change, makes the best of it, and usually ends up by becoming an expert.

July Monkey Year persons are very fine talkers. There is also a tendency for the person born under this sign to have a dual occupational life. For example: upon being graduated from medical school, he might open a restaurant or decide to become a chef. Then he might decide, at a later time, to go back to medicine.

Many persons born under this sign are attracted to persons born outside their own country. International marriages are common to this sign. Also, July Monkey Year persons rarely ever marry those people who have a similar ethnic or social background.

Food is very important in the life of a July Monkey Year person. He is very knowledgeable in this area. Persons born under this sign make the best chefs and cookbook writers.

Women of this sign are attracted to handsome, well-built men, even if they do not have good financial positions or social prestige.

Sometimes, the July Monkey Year person will hold poor opinions of others and hold them in contempt. He should work to eliminate this trait.

Women of this sign do best with males born in the month of March during the Year of the Horse or February during the Year of the Rabbit; also with men born in any month of a Dragon or Rat Year.

Men born in July of a Monkey Year should marry August Sheep Year women. Females born in August of a Dragon or Rat Year would also make good partners.

Both men and women should be careful of persons born in the Year of the Snake or Boar.

The Year of the Monkey—August

Those persons born in the month of August during the Year of the Monkey usually carry their duties through, no matter what.

August Monkey Year persons have special talents in the areas of planning and should work toward appropriate positions. They do especially well in advertising or as city and government planners.

Persons born under this sign have an innocent, childlike appearance that they carry throughout their lives.

August Monkey Year persons have a good sense of art and can do detailed work easily. They also work well with numbers and figures, solving the most difficult problems with ease.

Women of this sign have a healthy outlook on life; they have a good philosophy. Rarely does one find August Monkey Year women hanging around bars or seeking material pleasures.

It is very easy for an August Monkey Year person to make a decision, as he usually possesses innate common sense. He is the most practical of his sign.

Men born under this sign should marry November Boar or March Ox Year females.

Women should marry May Monkey or August Cock Year males. Those men born in the Year of the Tiger or Rat (any month) are also good companions for women of this sign.

Both men and women of this sign must be wary of persons born in the Year of the Snake.

Lyndon B. Johnson (August 27, 1908) is an August Monkey Year person. He was filled with a sense of duty, which he was able to carry out through his presidential office. His special talent lay in government planning. Decisions were easy for him, and they were usually practical.

The Year of the Monkey—September

Those persons born in the month of September during the Year of the Monkey are the most tense of their sign. They become very upset before any kind of test or examination. Usually, however, this nervousness is just the thing needed to propel the September Monkey Year person to success.

Persons born under this sign can have great success in life, and even become famous if they are left to follow their own course. Too much attention from others, even if they are trying to help, can make the September Monkey Year person so nervous and upset that he will be unable to function.

Women born in the month of September during the Year of the Monkey are usually quite nervous and affect habits such as pulling down their skirts to cover their knees, adjusting their blouses, checking to see that all buttons and pins are secure. This innocent behavior is usually an asset to September Monkey Year women, as it attracts many men.

Self-confidence and self-assurance are NOT attributes of this sign and must be constantly worked on by September Monkey Year persons. September Monkey Year persons, for all their negative qualities, are needed in society for their natural skills, of which there are many.

Men born under this sign should marry either December Horse or October Sheep Year females.

Women born in September of a Monkey Year do best with May or June Rabbit Year men. Another good corresponding sign would be August Sheep Year males or those males born in any month of the Rat Year.

Both men and women must be careful of those persons born in either the Year of the Boar or the Year of the Tiger.

The Year of the Monkey—October

Those persons born in the month of October during the Year of the Monkey are the most honest of their sign. They also work very hard and are most quick at whatever it is they wish to accomplish.

October Monkey Year persons never rest. Even on weekends they will take a car or a train to the nearest town and seek out bargain places and things to buy or see.

There is a tendency for the October Monkey Year person, when he is in a conversation, to be a bit selfish. They are interested in getting their points across and not in listening to the other side.

October Monkey Year persons should not become involved in employment situations that are restrictive or tight-scheduled. They are also not good in detailed work.

October Monkey Year people have a great thirst for knowledge, and they read, see, and learn things about countless subjects. Usually, however, it is difficult for them to impart this knowledge, as their language is not too sophisticated.

Women of this sign should marry men who were born in the month of August or September during the Year of the Ox or any Rat Year male. Males born in any month of the Year of the Rabbit also make good mates for this sign.

October Monkey Year males do best with March or February Boar Year females. They also are a good match for anyone born in the Year of the Rabbit.

The Year of the Monkey—November

Those persons born in the month of November during the Year of the Monkey are said to be the revolutionaries of their sign. They are always going after that which is new. November Monkey Year persons hate restrictions of any kind and must have freedom in their life or they suffer.

November Monkey Year persons make excellent writers and teachers. They have innate knowledge that propels them to success early in life.

Persons born in November of a Monkey Year are said to be the erratic geniuses of their sign. They are usually clever and most adroit in big-scale operations.

November Monkey Year males do best with women born in the Year of the Dragon, especially May and June Dragon Year females.

Females of this sign should marry men born in the Year of the Rabbit, Sheep, or the Rat (any month).

Both men and women born in November of a Monkey Year should not marry those born in the Year of the Tiger or the Year of the Boar.

There is a tendency for the November Monkey Year person to develop digestive trouble after his late twenties, and he must be careful to avoid this.

Virgil Thomson (November 25, 1896) is a typical November Monkey Year male. He is a true revolutionary in his music, always seeking new avenues of expression. His work is nonrestrictive and truly shows Thomson's need for freedom. He is an erratic genius.

The Year of the Monkey—December

Those persons born in the month of December during the Year of the Monkey are said to waste not one moment of their lives. They put every second of time to useful activity. They are also the most flexible of their cycle.

December Monkey Year persons are most harmonious with others and usually involve themselves with employment situations that bring pleasure to others, such as acting, singing, professional sports, and cooking.

Persons born under this sign work very hard, and when they play, they play just as hard. They are able to separate completely their business and home life.

Men born in December during the Year of the Monkey are great admirers of women. They know how to treat a woman and are most respectful toward them.

Women of this sign are extremely healthy and fertile. They usually have many children.

Men born under this sign should marry April Horse or September Boar Year women.

Females of this sign do best with either December Rabbit or December Sheep Year men as well as any Rat Year man.

Both men and women of this sign should be careful of anyone born in the Year of the Tiger.

THE YEAR OF THE COCK

General Traits

Persons born in the Year of the Cock are most enthusiastic. They can be extremely brave when it is called for. Cock Year persons have a tendency to be somewhat eccentric, and they must be careful of this characteristic in the business world. There is a deep-rooted selfishness in Cock Year persons that must be overcome. They will also say anything that comes into their minds. Cock Year persons are meditative and are the loners of the Oriental Zodiac.

The Year of the Cock—January

Those persons born in the month of January during the Year of the Cock are on the cusp of the previous sign, the Monkey, and should look into the aspects of that sign, especially December Monkey.

January Cock Year persons are quick-thinking and intelligent, two aspects of their personality that are not immediately evident. They do make good impressions on others and are very well liked.

Persons born in January of a Cock Year are the "big talkers" of their sign. Usually, their actions do not follow their words.

They make the best diplomats and do well in politics as well.

In matters of the heart, January Cock Year persons are cool, and even if they are deeply in love with someone, they will not show it on the surface.

Travel is most important in the lives of January Cock Year persons, especially intercontinental travel. Before their middle age, January Cock Year persons have usually done a great deal of traveling.

Men born in January of a Cock Year should marry November Ox, August Horse, or July Snake Year females.

January Cock Year females do best with those men born in the Year of the Dog (any month) or December Horse Year males.

Both males and females of this sign should not marry anyone born in the Year of the Rabbit.

The Year of the Cock—February

Those persons born in the month of February during the Year of the Cock love freedom. They spend much of their lives searching for this freedom. Those around them feel that the February Cock person is selfish because of this.

February Cock Year persons never compromise, even if it is to their own advantage in business or personal relationships.

Persons born under this sign tend to be far too critical of themselves. They are perpetually saying, "Why didn't I do it that way?" "If only I could do it over again."

February Cock Year persons do very well in small businesses. They should have their own shops or small enterprises, which will afford them the freedom they desire.

Persons born in February of a Cock Year like sports clothes rather than formal attire. They love leather goods and unusual materials.

February Cock Year persons hate tradition, as they are the most modern of their cycle. They always seek out the new and different, in clothes, eating places, or companions.

February Cock Year persons are loyal to their lovers. They will even follow a lover after the romance has broken up.

Men of this sign do best with August Rat Year women. They also do well with females born in any month during the Year of the Snake.

February Cock Year women should marry June Dragon or September Boar Year males.

Both men and women of this sign should be careful when in the company of those persons born in the Year of the Dog or Rabbit.

The Year of the Cock—March

Those persons born in the month of March during the Year of the Cock are the most idealistic of their sign. They live by the adage "Right is right!"

March Cock Year persons are extremely clean and demand cleanliness in everything. They make a very good first impression on others and are able to make those around them feel relaxed and at ease.

Persons born under this sign are affectionate and tend to be jealous in matters of the heart.

It is said in the Orient that when a March Cock Year person tries to help others he is usually deeply hurt by the very people he is helping. This occurs especially in employment situations where the March Cock Year person owns or runs the business. He will have a good deal of trouble with the people he hires.

If the March Cock Year person is the oldest child in the family, he will be most successful. Careers for people under this sign are varied and many. They make especially good government officials.

March Cock Year persons are usually busy for the major part of their life. They are also most devoted to their work, no matter what it is.

Men of this sign should marry those persons born in the Year of the Rabbit, especially September Rabbit Year women.

March Cock Year females do best with an August Dragon Year male. Ox Year males (all months) are also good.

Both men and women of this sign should be careful of those persons born in the Year of the Dog or the Year of the Rat.

The Year of the Cock—April

Those persons born in April during the Year of the Cock possess cheerful personalities. They usually have great senses of humor and are the jokesters of their cycle. April Cock Year persons are the most easygoing and kindly characters.

Persons born in this month have a strong desire to help others. They make excellent nurses, doctors, social workers, or psychiatrists.

April Cock Year persons are not demanding and expect very little from life. As long as they have a roof over their head and food in their stomach, they can be content.

April Cock Year persons are intelligent and usually have much self-control except in money matters. They are able to make money, but it has a tendency to go out as soon as it is earned.

April Cock Year persons should get into businesses where there is speculation, such as dealing in stocks and bonds. They make the best promoters and would even do well at gambling.

Sex is most important to a person born in April of a Cock Year. After adulthood, if they do not learn control in this area, some trouble could ensue.

April Cock Year persons love their children. They usually have a good family life if they do not become involved in any extramarital affairs.

Men of this sign do best with women born in the Year of the Snake, especially September or December Snake Year women.

Women of this sign should marry December Sheep Year men. They also do well with persons born in the Year of the Dragon (any month).

Both male and female April Cock Year persons should not become attached to anyone born in the Year of the Rabbit or the Year of the Rat.

Both Jean-Paul Belmondo (April 9, 1933) and Peter Ustinov (April 16, 1921) are typical April Cock Year males. Each has a very pronounced sense of humor and is said to be easygoing and kindly. Each man has been busy since his career started, and both are most devoted to their work. They are also both extremely intelligent and express great self-control.

The Year of the Cock—May

Persons born in the month of May during the Year of the Cock possess the mildest nature of their cycle. They are also the most consistent in all matters, business or pleasure.

A vast amount of trust is placed in a May Cock Year person. He tends to get a position where he deals with money. Even in club activities, outside of work, he is asked to be treasurer.

May Cock Year persons are sometimes too careful in respect to what others think. They worry over what others are thinking or saying about them. For this reason, the May Cock Year person tends to be a loner and does not usually have too many friends. They do not trust others and prefer to have one or two close friends.

They love books, and many May Cock Year persons will seek jobs that in some way are connected to books (editors, librarians, or writers).

In matters of love, they tend to be cool, almost indifferent. May Cock Year persons are hardly ever overpassionate.

Persons born under this sign must watch out for stomach and digestive diseases.

Women of this sign do best with men born in the Year of the Snake, especially in November. They also do well with February Dragon Year males.

Males born in May of a Cock Year should marry January Dog or June Ox Year females.

Both males and females born in a May Cock Year should be cautious of persons born in the Year of the Rabbit.

The Year of the Cock—June

Persons born in the month of June during the Year of the Cock are the most sensitive of this cycle. They get angry or depressed quicker than others because of this sensitivity.

June Cock Year persons always have ideas that are new and formative. It is said in the Orient that June Cock Year persons are good planners with great ideas but that they need others to see that the plans are carried out.

Persons born under this sign tend to be sarcastic when they speak, and they also like to gossip a bit.

June Cock Year persons usually have good relationships with their family. They tend to be spoiled by their parents. For this reason, they don't like to be alone.

June Cock Year persons can be a bit superstitious and usually carry some kind of luck piece or charm. They are also very religious.

Whatever the trend in style (hair or fashion), the June Cock Year person will adapt to it. Usually, he looks good in the latest style.

June Cock Year persons make good stage directors, producers, and writers and also excel in journalism.

Persons of this sign always try to do more than they can and become depressed and disappointed when they cannot fulfill their obligations.

Men of this sign do best with either August or September Rabbit Year women, also with August Rat Year females.

June Cock Year females should marry either September Tiger or October Rat Year men. Also favorable are April Sheep Year men.

If persons of this sign have many children, one will become famous.

The Year of the Cock—July

Persons born in the month of July during the Year of the Cock are the busiest of their cycle. Their brain is quick, and ideas come continuously to the July Cock Year person.

July Cock Year persons usually have a good childhood and are well protected by their parents until their twentieth birthday. After leaving their parents' home, the July Cock Year person experiences much hardship and difficulty. His own success does not usually come until after his thirtieth birthday.

The love of a July Cock Year person is deep, sensitive, and everlasting. He does expect beauty in his lovers and will seek out those who possess both inward and outward beauty.

July Cock Year persons not only have ideas but are usually able to carry them out. They do have a tendency to tire easily and need time to replenish their depleted energy.

Persons of this sign are attracted to that which is new in the world, whether it be fashion, art, or a new philosophy.

If a July Cock Year person gets mad, he will not talk to the one he is angry with for days. Wives or husbands of people born under this sign, therefore, have difficult times in their life.

The July Cock Year person should have a speculative job. He does well in the export-import business. Journalism and publishing suit the July Cock Year person too.

Women born in July of a Cock Year do best with persons born in any month of the Year of the Dragon. A March or December Ox Year male is also a good match.

July Cock Year males do best with March or April Horse and August Boar Year females.

Both men and women of this sign should be wary of those persons born in the Year of the Dog or Rabbit.

The Year of the Cock—August

Persons born in the month of August during the Year of the Cock are the liberals of their cycle. They are broad-minded and are usually charming.

August Cock Year persons do not like discipline and are therefore a bit weak-willed. They also give in to temptation easily.

Persons of this sign do very good office work and usually develop excellent social contacts. All the fields of art (especially literature) could hold a career for an August Cock Year person.

Women of this sign are nymphlike, and most men are attracted to August Cock Year females.

The liberal mind of the August Cock Year person can become quite eccentric, and this prevents him from having complete, fulfilling relationships with others. August Cock Year persons always think that they are right and that they know exactly what they are doing.

Women of this sign should marry September or October Tiger or June Dragon Year males.

August Cock Year men do best with women born in August of a Monkey Year or in any month of an Ox Year.

Both males and females born in August of a Cock Year should be careful of those born in the Year of the Rat.

There is a tendency toward vitamin deficiency in persons born under this sign.

The Year of the Cock—September

Persons born in the month of September during the Year of the Cock are the individualists of their sign. They do not like to follow others, whether it be in clothes, tastes, or thinking. They have a need to remain independent! There is a uniqueness about September Cock Year persons because of their independence.

September Cock Year persons have unusual ideas. They are usually brave and will try anything. They should get jobs that suit their individualism. Many designers have been born under this sign.

Women of this sign are well liked at their place of business. September Cock Year women usually have beautiful eyes.

The fortunes of September Cock Year persons resemble the waves of the ocean; sometimes they are rich, sometimes poor. September Cock Year persons should save for that rainy day which will eventually come to them.

Men born under this sign do best with November Horse, June Boar or April Ox Year women.

September Cock Year females should marry Monkey Year men, especially March Monkey Year men.

Both men and women do not usually get along with anyone born in the sign of the Rabbit.

The Year of the Cock—October

Persons born in the month of October during the Year of the Cock are the most mysterious of their sign. Even close friends of October Cock Year persons do not know all about those born under this sign.

October Cock Year persons are very honest, and they possess kind, gentle hearts. It is said in the Orient that October Cock Year persons do not like even to kill insects.

Persons of this sign do have strong wills, and they are most competitive in their line of work. They usually get good positions by gradually moving up the ladder of success.

The mysterious quality of October Cock Year persons affords them unusual employment opportunities, such as international spying. They are able to change their lives completely, taking nothing with them from the old life. They usually keep to themselves and have few friends and acquaintances.

Women born in October of a Cock Year are usually pursued by many men. Their secretive, mysterious nature becomes a challenge for most men. October Cock Year women do have a habit of complaining about their lovers' weak points, however, and they then lose out on romance after some time.

Men of this sign do best with July or August Dragon Year women.

Women born in October of a Cock Year do best with men born in the Year of the Snake, especially November Snake Year males.

Both men and women of this sign should be careful of persons born under their own sign, the Year of the Cock.

The Year of the Cock—November

Persons born in November during the Year of the Cock retain a childlike quality throughout their entire life. They never lose the curiosity of a child and approach everything they do with childlike enthusiasm. November Cock Year persons tend to be a bit too naive, owing to their childlike ways, and must be careful not to be hurt because of this.

November Cock Year persons are simple and uncomplicated. When they are forty years old, they will read adventure stories and those books they read as teen-agers, and they will be thrilled all over again.

Persons born under this sign do not understand teasing and will strike out in real anger at anyone who attempts to tease them.

Women of this sign are very sexual and have a tendency to be a bit promiscuous, although it is through naiveté that this occurs.

November Cock Year men are the opposite of women of this sign. Sex is usually not important to males of this sign, and their love is most simple. Many November Cock Year men remain single throughout their lives. When they do marry, however, they have good, warm family relationships.

Males born under this sign should marry April Dragon or February Boar Year females.

Women of this sign do best with July Horse or December Year males. Persons born in the Year of the Snake or Ox are also well matched to November Cock Year women.

The Year of the Cock—December

Those persons born in the month of December during the Year of the Cock are cheerful and understanding. They are very complimentary to others, who in turn like to do things for December Cock Year people.

There is a tendency for December Cock Year persons to take advantage of others; they should be careful of this trait or they will lose out, both in business and in their home life.

December Cock Year persons know quite a bit about law. If they so choose, December Cock Year persons make excellent lawyers. Their judgment is very fine, and they should be involved in employment situations where this judgment will be put to use. Other good employment possibilities would be journalism or politics.

It is said in the Orient that December Cock Year persons make the best mates, for they are enjoyable and always seek the new and different.

Women of this sign are very knowledgeable and put their knowledge to use.

Men born in December of a Cock Year should marry either a July or August Boar Year person or people born in any month during the Year of the Dragon.

December Cock Year females do best with Dog Year males, especially October, or July Ox Year men.

Both men and women born under this sign should not become involved with anyone born in the Year of the Rat or Rabbit.

THE YEAR OF THE DOG

General Traits

Persons born in the Year of the Dog are most sincere and completely honest. They are also the faultfinders of the Oriental Zodiac and will criticize anything they feel is wrong. Dog Year persons make excellent friends, however, because of their unyielding loyalty. They will never betray a friend. There is a tendency for the Dog Year person to be somewhat stubborn and a bit eccentric. Emotionally, Dog Year persons maintain their cool.

The Year of the Dog—January

Those persons born in January during the Year of the Dog possess mild temperaments. They are most affectionate toward those they come in contact with.

Being that this sign is on the cusp of the preceding sign, the Cock, January Dog Year persons might be a bit like persons born under that sign, especially December Cock Year.

January Dog Year persons must have everything in order, at home or in their place of business.

Persons born under this sign put great effort into any work they undertake. They are not particularly lucky, succeeding mainly through their own endeavors.

January Dog Year persons do very well in publishing, editing, scholastic work, or engineering; if they apply themselves, they can be successful in almost any area.

Women of this sign should marry men who are quite a bit older than they are. Happiness will come to those women who do have an older man.

January Dog Year persons become very upset if they go somewhere and the place is not in order. They see every bit of dust or dirt in another person's home, and during the course of the conversation, they will let their host know, in some way, that their home is not being kept up to par.

Men born in January of a Dog Year do best with either April Dragon or October Cock Year women.

Women of this sign should marry either February Sheep or May Cock Year persons or anyone born in the Year of the Rabbit.

Both men and women must be wary of persons born in the Year of the Sheep.

The Year of the Dog—February

Those persons born in the month of February during the Year of the Dog are extremely extroverted and most cheerful. They also possess sharp judgment. They do lose out by acting on their first impressions, which are not always correct.

February Dog Year persons have many small failures in their lives. When they occur, they should get away from whatever they are attempting to accomplish for a while, and return to it later; then they will be successful.

Persons born under this sign are well liked by others and usually have many friends. Others hold February Dog Year persons in high regard and consider them fine friends. It is desirable to have a February Dog Year person as a close friend.

February Dog Year persons do well in occupations that deal directly with money—banking, or investing.

February Dog Year persons care a great deal about their appearance, and both men and women spend time, effort, and money on clothes, hair styles, and other externals.

February Dog Year females are very good wives and mothers. They create a fine family atmosphere.

Men born under this sign should marry February Horse Year or December Sheep Year females.

February Dog Year females do best with May Tiger men. Males born in the month of June and July of a Horse Year also make good husbands for women of this sign.

Both males and females born in February during the Year of the Dog should be careful of anyone born in the Year of the Ox or the Year of the Cock.

The Year of the Dog—March

Persons born in the month of March during the Year of the Dog are said to have a double personality. They are changeable and sometimes erratic. March Dog Year persons keep their home life separate from their business life.

March Dog Year persons possess excellent business minds. They do well in occupations such as writing and any cultural or artistic activity. They make fine designers.

There is a tendency for persons born under this sign to inherit money; they must be careful, for they could lose it all in speculative business situations.

Persons born under this sign possess sharp tongues, and they do look for faults in others.

Women of this sign become depressed quite often. They then revert to their other personality, changing their style of clothes, their perfume, or even their boyfriends. They can be quite erratic.

March Dog Year men do best with October Rabbit or January Boar Year females. An October Rabbit Year female would also be a good choice for men of this sign.

March Dog Year women should marry either August Rat Year or October Sheep Year men.

Both men and women of this sign should not become involved with persons born in the Year of the Cock or the Year of the Dragon.

The Year of the Dog—April

Persons born in April during the Year of the Dog are the most logical of their cycle, at least in their thinking. Sometimes, they will purposely go against their logical thinking and act illogically, causing those around them confusion because of this duality.

April Dog Year persons are passionate in their romances. They also possess much energy. Lovers of people born under this sign are usually exhausted.

April Dog Year persons cannot stand injustice of any kind. If they come across injustice in their lives, they will not rest until the situation is corrected in a rightful manner.

April Dog Year persons do well in employment situations connected to big business organizations or trading firms. They do not do well in their own business.

It is said in the Orient that April Dog Year persons dream too much and have their head in the clouds. If they can bring themselves down and look closely at their abilities, then they will have much success.

Women of this sign do best with men whose jobs are of the escalating kind, under the raise-and-promotion system.

April Dog Year males do best with July Dragon Year or October Ox Year females.

April Dog Year women should marry January Boar, February Horse, or May Dragon Year men.

Both men and women must be careful of anyone born in the Year of the Sheep.

The Year of the Dog—May

Persons born in the month of May during the Year of the Dog are the most quick-thinking of their cycle. They usually possess calm, simple, direct personalities.

May Dog Year persons must put tremendous effort into their work if they are to be successful. They usually move ahead at a very slow pace, little by little.

Persons of this sign tend to be subtle in their approach to others and work with finesse. They make excellent secretaries and do well in any kind of plan making.

Men of this sign are loyal to their mates or lovers. They are truly one-woman men.

May Dog Year persons have a deep sense of duty and have very good relationships with others. They get other people's confidence and will keep secrets.

Both men and women of this sign tend to have sensitive skin and must be careful not to come into contact with those things which will cause them to break out.

May Dog Year women make good wives and like to serve their husbands.

May Dog Year men should marry either June Dog Year females or persons born in any month during the Year of the Horse.

May Dog Year females do best with April Dragon, May Sheep, or December Boar Year men.

Both men and women of this sign should not affiliate themselves with anyone born in the Year of the Ox.

The Year of the Dog—June

Those persons born in the month of June during the Year of the Dog are very sociable. There are many factors in the character of the June Dog Year person that will bring about his success—most important, great physical and extraordinary mental power.

June Dog Year persons are liked by their bosses and usually get good promotions. But the promotions will not last if they don't apply themselves completely to their business situations. June Dog Year persons are like unpolished gems. They must constantly work at the polishing and honing of their nature.

Travel is important in the lives of June Dog Year persons, and they usually do quite a bit of it.

June Dog Year persons have countless acquaintances but few close friends. It would behoove them to develop one or two close relationships.

Throughout their lives, June Dog Year persons have very high expenses and find it difficult to save money.

June Dog Year persons excel in the retail business, or in any kind of company dealing in natural resources. Men of this sign will sometimes join in the business of their in-laws and become quite successful.

Women born in June during a Dog Year should marry January Ox Year or May Dog Year males.

June Dog Year men do best with January Dragon Year or April or July Tiger Year females.

Both men and women of this sign should not marry anyone born in the Year of the Sheep.

The Year of the Dog—July

Persons born in the month of July during the Year of the Dog are the most open of their cycle. They also will complete any job they set out to accomplish. Others find it most convenient to have July Dog Year persons working for them.

There is a tendency for the July Dog Year person to be too

honestly open. They cannot keep a secret and will sometimes even tell others the innermost secrets of their family life.

Persons of this sign are sensitive and lead very colorful lives. They usually have many friends. Even the love life of July Dog Year persons is varied and colorful. They do tire easily, however.

Women born in July of a Dog Year tend to be cute rather than beautiful. They must be careful of developing skin diseases.

Persons born under this sign are not materialistic and seem to be able to have money whenever they need it.

July Dog Year persons talk a bit too much and must watch this habit, which can be destructive for them.

Men born under this sign should marry anyone born in the Year of the Dragon, especially March Dragon Year females.

Women born under this sign do best with either March or April Tiger Year men.

Both men and women of this sign should not marry anyone born in the Year of the Cock.

Alexandre Dumas (July 24, 1802) was a July Dog Year male. He was most sensitive and very open. Dumas led a most varied and colorful life. His friends were numberless, and it is said that Dumas found it hard to keep a secret.

The Year of the Dog—August

Persons born in the month of August during the Year of the Dog possess a cool nature. They are the outsiders of their cycle, hating to be involved. August Dog Year people never take chances, both in business and personal life. If they are not 100 percent sure that something will work, August Dog Year persons will not attempt it.

Usually, August Dog Year persons are contemplative and will not act before giving the situation deep thought. They rarely have big failures in their lives because of this. However, they also miss out on situations that could become advantageous for them.

August Dog Year persons like creativity and should become involved in a business where there is a chance for them to be creative, such as television or motion pictures.

Usually, the August Dog Year person has good family ties. In fact, ties with sisters and brothers can be so strong that outsiders feel the August Dog Year person cares only about his family.

August Dog Year persons truly love their children and will do everything for them to have a good education.

Women of this sign do best with either April Horse Year or November Rabbit Year males.

August Dog Year men should marry December Horse Year females. Those women born in the Year of the Rat, especially March Rat, would also be good for August Dog Year men.

Both men and women of this sign should not marry anyone born in the Year of the Sheep or the Year of the Ox.

The Year of the Dog—September

Persons born in the month of September during the Year of the Dog are the most disciplined of their sign. They never compromise. In human relationships, the September Dog Year person either loves or hates; he has no middle ground. If they are to be successful, September Dog Year persons should learn to control this extremism.

September Dog Year persons find it difficult to hide their true feelings or emotions. They tend to lose a lot of friends because of this.

Persons born under this sign should become involved in jobs that call for discipline or detail work. They do well in bank jobs and the stock exchange. They excel in institutional work.

September Dog Year persons are free and easygoing. They enjoy good times and attend many parties.

Persons born under this sign also have excellent, retentive memories. It is easy for them to memorize, and they make the best foreign-language students.

September Dog Year persons love to be the center of attention.

Women of this sign do best with December Horse or September Sheep Year males.

September Dog Year males should marry July Snake, March Dragon, or October Tiger Year women.

Both men and women should be careful of anyone born in the Year of the Cock.

The Year of the Dog—October

Persons born in the month of October during the Year of the Dog are the most honest and direct of their cycle. They are also kind and extremely clever.

October Dog Year persons are very intuitive and have ESP powers.

Persons of this sign are quick in summing up people, and they are usually correct. They will notice another person's good or bad points immediately.

October Dog Year persons are good with money matters and make excellent accountants. Usually, persons born under this sign will get into a business in which they are interested. They also excel in any kind of scholastic work.

When an October Dog Year person marries, it is usually for love. They need love in their lives and are quite romantic.

October Dog Year persons are conservative in most matters, whether it be clothes or spending money. However, they always look good and are well groomed.

Women of this sign do very well with those men born in the Year of the Snake, especially June Snake Year males. December Cock Year men are also most compatible for women of this sign.

Males born in October during the Year of the Dog do very well with July Snake Year or November Cock Year females.

Both men and women of this sign should not become involved with anyone born in the Year of the Sheep.

The Year of the Dog—November

Persons born in November during the Year of the Dog have tremendous fighting spirit. They can overcome practically any obstacle because of this strength, and they usually have many obstacles in their path.

November Dog Year persons lead a most private life. They do not like to be bothered and build an imaginary wall around themselves, rarely letting anyone inside their private circle. Usually, November Dog Year persons are not too sociable. Their life style and actions are cool.

November Dog Year persons excel in secretarial work or managerial positions.

Persons of this sign are not noted for small talk. However, they are able to handle others very well. They make excellent leaders in industry and large firms.

Men of this month have a tendency to be a bit untrustworthy in love matters.

Women born in November of a Dog Year think too much about their lovers. They do not say much to them, however, and this leads to difficulty in love relationships.

There is a tendency for the November Dog Year person to find fault with others and to criticize that which he feels is wrong.

November Dog Year women do best with men born in the Year of the Horse, especially August Horse Year males. A March Boar Year man is also a good mate.

November Dog Year men should be with December Rat Year women.

Both men and women of this sign should be careful of anyone born in the Year of the Sheep or the Year of the Cock.

The Year of the Dog—December

Persons born in the month of December during the Year of the Dog are the romanticists of their cycle. They are also most sympathetic toward others. This giving attitude makes those around December Dog Year persons want to do things for them.

December Dog Year persons are also extremely honest.

They cannot hide anything, even those things that best remain hidden.

Persons born under this sign need love in their lives. They cannot survive without it. In fact, love matters sometimes prove to be overwhelming for the overromantic December Dog Year person.

Honor is important to December Dog persons. They cannot endure insult to their honor. December Dog Year persons have great pride.

December Dog Year persons are very competitive. They do well in scholastic work, as a teacher or principal. Writing and music are also areas of interest that the December Dog Year person could pursue with success.

Justice is most important in the lives of persons born under this sign. They become highly incensed by anything that is unjust.

Women of this sign do well with January Rabbit Year men. Males born in the Year of the Horse are also well suited for the December Dog Year woman.

December Dog Year males should marry August Horse or April Rat Year females. Anyone born in the Year of the Tiger would also be a good match for men of this sign.

Both males and females of the December Dog Year sign should be wary of persons born in either the Year of the Cock or the Year of the Ox.

THE YEAR OF THE BOAR

General Traits

Persons born in the Year of the Boar are the most mannerly and indeed the most gallant of the Oriental Zodiac. They are also short-tempered and can be impulsive. It is wise never to anger a Boar Year person. They possess a strong will that cannot be changed or broken, an inner strength impossible to overcome. Boar Year persons will work at a task until it is accomplished. They have tremendous staying power. Boar Year persons are perpetual students and are very honest in all matters.

The Year of the Boar—January

Persons born in the month of January during the Year of the Boar are steady and keep straight on any given path. There are effects of the previous sign, the Dog, this month being a cusp sign.

Money is usually not important in the lives of January Boar Year persons. They are not good at money matters, which is not true for the other eleven Boar signs.

Law, in all its aspects, would be an excellent line of endeavor for the January Boar Year person to pursue. January Boar Year persons are loyal to their jobs and usually keep them for long periods of time. Women of this sign, even after they marry, tend to hold onto their job.

January Boar Year persons mature earlier than other people. They usually have their first serious love affair in their teens. Women of this sign develop quite early, physically and mentally. Usually, women of a January Boar Year sign marry very early in life. They are excellent mood makers for romance.

January Boar Year persons have great fortitude. They will give all their strength to reach any goal, never straying from left or right until the task is accomplished. They will not give up even when exhausted.

Men of this sign do well with February Snake Year or April Dog Year women.

January Boar Year females should marry March Dog Year males. Persons born in the Year of the Rabbit (any month) also make good companions for the January Boar Year person.

Both men and women of this sign should not marry anyone born in the Year of the Monkey.

The Year of the Boar—February

Persons born in the month of February during the Year of the Boar are said to be the helpers of their cycle. Usually, they go into businesses that serve others in some way. They can greatly benefit from serving others as ministers, doctors, or in key management positions that cater to the public.

There is a tendency for others to want to take advantage of February Boar Year persons, and they must be careful of this, especially when choosing close friends.

February Boar Year persons should not depend on others; rather they should make their own decisions, forging ahead by their own efforts. They will be more successful if they follow their own impressions.

There is a tendency for February Boar Year persons to be a bit materialistic and too desirous in sexual and material matters such as clothes and art collections. If they do not learn control, this aspect of their nature will ruin them.

Persons of this sign tire easily of human relationships and need time to be on their own, completely away from everyone else.

February Boar Year persons are short-tempered and yet hate arguments and quarrels of any kind. If goaded beyond endurance, they will become violent.

Women of this sign do best with October Tiger or November Cock Year men.

Males born in the month of February during a Boar Year should marry either March Rabbit Year or November Monkey Year females.

Both men and women of this sign should be careful of relationships with those persons born in the Year of the Snake.

The Year of the Boar—March

Persons born in the month of March during the Year of the Boar have a great thirst for knowledge. They usually know many things about vast numbers of subjects. March Boar Year persons are continually studying. The knowledge they acquire about all the subjects in which they are interested, however, is usually surface material.

March Boar Year persons do not listen to others, preferring to go along on their own. They never ask advice but are usually asked for it. They trust their inner feelings on things and are usually correct. When they fail, for instance in business, it is usually a major disaster.

A March Boar Year person has a tendency to take over his father's business or to inherit family money. Usually, when he does take over the business, he develops it further, with much success.

Men of this sign tend to be passionate. They do not speak much, but when they do talk, everything comes out at one time. One who is verbally attacked by a March Boar Year male will never forget it.

Persons of this sign have a great sense of color and fashion. They usually have modern taste in all things.

Men of this sign do well with November Snake and February Tiger Year females. They also do well with persons born in the Year of the Rat (any month).

March Boar Year women should marry October Dragon Year men or men born in the Year of the Rabbit.

Both men and women of this sign should not marry anyone born in the Year of the Monkey or their own sign, the Boar.

The Year of the Boar—April

Persons born in the month of April during the Year of the Boar are the sophisticates of their sign. They also possess good character. Their taste in all things is exquisite, and they tend to be connoisseurs.

April Boar Year persons usually marry late in life because of an early ill-fated love affair that hurts them deeply. They have many friends and acquaintances. The April Boar Year person will lose many of them, however, owing to an irritating quality of not being able to make up his mind.

Men of this sign have lots of energy and fight in them. They will work on a job until it is completed, never giving up, no matter how difficult.

April Boar Year persons never ask for outside help, preferring to do everything themselves. It is even difficult to get them to see a doctor.

April Boar Year persons are most gallant and chivalrous. They are also very honest. If they can control the other aspects of their sign, these three attributes will take them far.

Women of this sign should marry men born in either September of a Dragon Year or March of a Tiger Year.

April Boar Year males do best with May Snake Year or September Sheep Year females.

Both men and women born in April during the Year of the Boar must be careful of relationships with persons born in the Year of the Monkey or their own sign.

Vladimir Nabokov (April 23, 1899) is an April Boar Year male. He possesses the "fighting" spirit of this sign and has worked against many odds for success in his writing. He is gallant, chivalrous, and honest and his taste, which is reflected in his works, is fine. He did marry late in life.

The Year of the Boar—May

Persons born in the month of May during the Year of the Boar are both affectionate and kind to their loved ones. They are also very honest.

May Boar Year persons never compromise. They will listen to others quietly and then make their own decision on matters.

Persons born in May of a Boar Year are not leaders. They are much better at carrying out orders than at giving them.

Success does not come easily to May Boar Year persons. It seems that they must work twice as hard as others to reach any goal.

There is a saying in the Orient that May Boar Year persons like to be loved rather than to love.

May Boar Year persons like outdoor sports and activities such as swimming, walking, or cycling. Professional sports would be a good choice for the May Boar Year person.

May Boar Year persons usually marry people from a completely opposite social situation than the one they were born into.

Men of this sign should marry January Horse or March Sheep Year females.

May Boar Year women do best with August Ox Year or August Tiger Year males.

Both males and females of this sign would do well to be wary of anyone born in the Year of the Snake or the Year of the Monkey.

The Year of the Boar—June

Persons born in June during the Year of the Boar possess sensitive personalities. They tend to let small things upset or worry them. They are the most anxious of their cycle and never seem to be able to stop worrying about tomorrow.

June Boar Year persons usually are slow starters, especially in business, but they are able to advance later, picking up both speed and accuracy as they go along.

Women of this sign like to read and to gather knowledge. They do not enjoy being merely a housewife and will seek outside work or diversion.

Both men and women of this sign should be in businesses that cater to females, such as hair styling, cosmetics, cooking, or running a boutique.

Men of this sign are quite masculine in their tastes. They like sports and traveling to interesting places, such as Africa.

Marriage for a person of this sign is usually fraught with quarrels and upsets; however, the quarreling often has good results. Steam is let off and by the next day all is forgotten. There is a tendency for second marriages.

It is difficult for the young June Boar Year person to make a decision, and they must work to overcome this or else lose out.

Women of this sign should marry September Rabbit or September Cock Year men.

Males born in June of a Boar Year do best with September Snake or December Boar Year females.

The Year of the Boar—July

Persons born in the month of July during the Year of the Boar are extremely harmonious with others. They tend to feel obligated to their friends and relatives.

Since July Boar Year persons have a tendency to be a bit lazy, success comes to them only if they go into a business they are interested in or a field that proves exciting and challenging to them.

July Boar Year persons will never gossip about others and will usually not be gossiped about in return. Their reputations are usually unsullied.

Persons of this sign do well in their own business, especially small shops that sell antiques, modern clothes, or boutique items. They also excel in show business and in most of the other arts.

Sometimes, July Boar Year persons have a strong love in their youth that does not work out. If this happens, there is a tendency for the couple to meet years later and rekindle their youthful romance.

Persons of this sign are quite impulsive and must be careful of this, or they will lose out.

July Boar Year men should marry November Sheep Year or April Monkey Year females.

Women of this sign do best with either June Ox Year or August Horse Year males.

Both males and females of this sign should be careful of those persons born in the Year of the Snake.

The Year of the Boar—August

Persons born in the month of August during the Year of the Boar possess excellent judgment. They are also strong-willed and very spirited.

August Boar Year persons are very honest and always say

exactly what they feel. If they see something that bothers them in a person, they will let him know in no uncertain terms. Sometimes they hurt even close friends by this outspoken attitude.

August Boar Year persons make the best employers and know how to use their responsibility when they become employers or managers.

August Boar Year persons have strong physical power, but they tire quite easily by exerting themselves too often.

Persons of this sign take on extra responsibility, such as caring for an elderly loved one. In employment situations they will sometimes do work that has been allotted to others.

Many obstacles are placed in the path of August Boar Year persons, and they must work hard to ascend the business ladder.

There is a tendency for August Boar Year persons to have difficult times with their in-laws.

Women of this sign do well with July Cock Year or January Tiger Year men.

August Boar Year males should marry April Monkey, November Sheep, or December Horse Year females.

Both men and women should not marry anyone born in their own sign, the Boar, or those born in the Year of the Snake.

The Year of the Boar—September

Persons born in the month of September during the Year of the Boar possess a fine, delicate sense of all things. They apply themselves completely to whatever they are involved in.

There is a tendency for September Boar Year persons to expend too much energy in their efforts. They find it difficult to recoup this lost energy.

August Boar Year persons get stimulation from others. They excel in any kind of group activity, whether it be in business or in their private lives.

Persons born in September of a Boar Year are excellent craftsmen and can make careers in this area.

Hobbies are important in the lives of September Boar Year males. They like miniature models and trains.

September Boar Year persons are gallant and possess a pure nature. They also have pronounced fortitude and deep honesty. It is said in the Orient that one is indeed fortunate to have a September Boar Year person as a friend.

Women of this sign do best with men born in the Year of the Rat, especially July Rat males.

Men of this sign should marry June Sheep, February Cock, or January Monkey Year females.

Both men and women born in the month of September during a Boar Year should not marry anyone born in the Year of the Snake.

The Year of the Boar—October

Persons born in the month of October during the Year of the Boar are not in the least bit introverted, which seems to be a characteristic of the other months in the Boar Year sign. They are most cheerful and quite passionate.

October Boar Year persons are simple and direct in their human relationships. They tend to be a bit stingy and somewhat absentminded.

October Boar Year persons make many small mistakes. If they can correct these, they will have success in their lives.

Persons born under this sign do not usually like anything that is overdone. They wear simple, uncolorful clothes and do not like overdecorated living quarters.

October Boar Year persons like to gamble and will attend functions where there is gambling, such as bingo games and horse races.

October Boar Year persons do not usually have too many friends. However, when they do develop friendships, they keep them for the major part of their lives.

Persons of this sign are attracted to cheerful home-loving types and usually marry people who have these attributes.

Men of this sign should be with June Sheep Year or November Boar Year females.

Women born in the month of October during the Year of

the Boar do best with November Snake, July Rabbit, or April Tiger Year men.

Both men and women of this sign should not marry anyone born in the Year of the Monkey.

The Year of the Boar—November

Persons born in November during the Year of the Boar seek justice more than any others of their cycle. They have a great desire to help or protect others and do well in any employment that renders this kind of service.

November Boar Year persons do not like to compromise. They also have difficulty talking with others, because they fear they have a poor vocabulary.

It is said in the Orient that November Boar Year persons are not sociable. They do have a tendency to be a bit unstable in employment situations, gravitating back and forth. Usually this is because their bosses do not like them, for they ask too many questions and make too many suggestions. If they get a boss who appreciates an inquisitive, ever-growing mind, they will be able to make great progress in their work.

November Boar Year persons usually look much younger than they are. They are straight and direct when they do speak. November Boar Year persons are usually patient; they have their patience tested many times throughout their lives.

November Boar Year persons make good teachers, professors, writers, and the like.

When they marry, November Boar Year persons should choose mates who are strong both physically and mentally.

Women born under this sign do best with either January Horse Year or October Boar Year males.

November Boar Year males do best with a November Rat Year woman.

Both men and women of this sign should be careful of those people born in the Year of the Snake.

The Year of the Boar—December

Persons born in the month of December during the Year of the Boar possess a great deal of self-confidence. They also have enjoyable and pleasing personalities.

December Boar Year persons have strong judgment ability and always act on it. Sometimes their judgment is wrong, however; they must be careful of this, for it might do them harm in the long run.

They must also not let themselves become too self-confident. If they watch this aspect of their personalities, they will succeed.

December Boar Year persons will never take detours on their path to success. If an obstacle shows up in front of them, they face it with great fortitude, and this fighting spirit will usually do away with whatever is in their path.

Persons of this sign find it difficult to feel or sense what others are thinking. Men especially are not too understanding of their women and must work at being more understanding, or they will lose out.

If persons of this sign marry and utilize the talents of their mates in business, they will both be successful. They do very well in businesses of their own.

Women of this sign should marry June Boar Year or November Tiger Year males.

December Boar Year males do best with May Dog, September Snake, or August Sheep Year persons.

Both men and women of this sign should not marry anyone born in the Year of the Snake or the Year of the Monkey.

Maria Callas (December 4, 1923) is a typical December Boar Year person. She certainly expresses a self-confident aura. In fact, if anything, she was too self-confident, almost ruining her career. Madame Callas never took detours in her singing life, forging ahead, knocking over any obstacle in her path, with that great fighting spirit of hers. She also has strong judgment.

EPILOGUE

In early 1971 the world was shocked by the suicide of Yukio Mishima, the most noted novelist of modern-day Japan. The explanations for his choice of death have been many and various. Generally, it is believed that Mishima decided upon suicide to forcibly bring to the attention of the Japanese people his beliefs that their country was losing ground in keeping the traditions and maintaining the spirit of a changing land; that Japan would be destroyed if the people did not heed his call for a return to the ways of a feudalistic Japan.

Yukio Mishima committed the ancient ritual of hara-kiri, an act in itself which conjures up both fear and revulsion in the Western mind. Like much that occurs in Oriental culture, hara-kiri seems a direct contradiction to the meditative, quiet-speaking, well-mannered, disciplined, and beauty-loving peoples of that part of the world.

During my stay in the Orient, I discovered that even many of the most violent acts have a deeper, spiritual meaning. It isn't that life is held cheaply in the Orient, rather the soul is of most importance, placing the physical body in second or even third place. In the West, we feel that physical death is the climax, the end, the change into nothingness (regardless of how many different versions of Heaven and Hell, or the hereafter, are taught).

In the ancient ritual of hara-kiri, one kneels on the floor and, with a sharp dagger, inserts the blade beneath the right side of the rib cage. Pulling the blade directly across the stomach to the left side, it is then drawn upward into the heart.

Why, I asked, if one must die, even for loss of honor (the usual reason for hara-kiri) does it have to be so physical, so seemingly bloody. My question was answered. The drawing of the blade completely across the midriff and upward naturally opens up the stomach. Ancient Japanese belief teaches that the soul was located in the solar plexus, the pit of the stomach. Hara-kiri is actually the opening up of that part of the body to enable the spirit to be released, to fly more quickly to where it goes before its eventual return to earth in another body. It would be easier to stab oneself directly in the heart, but without hara-kiri, the soul might remain in the body.

Mishima's death has become a great debate in Japan. Many laugh at this method and shrug it off as a bit of insanity or extreme eccentricity. Countless others have taken a long hard look at themselves and their country, asking if they have not sacrificed spiritual qualities for the seemingly far more rewarding material satisfactions.

There is enough of the spiritual in Japan to yet overcome the ever expanding material ways. Whether it be astrology, Buddhism, or the other beliefs in various aspects of the occult, one finds the Japanese culture still much involved in the perfection of the spirit, the advancement of the soul.

I think I have pointed out the value in Westerners knowing that reincarnation and astrology exist. I have seen even the most downtrodden, lost soul come into enlightenment through his realization of reincarnation.

When an Oriental practices the truths of reincarnation and astrology, he does not blindly and carelessly rush into the business of living. He becomes more aware and cautious of his relationships with others. Knowing of the effects of Karma, an Oriental who is involved in the teachings of reincarnation does not deliberately do harm to any soul, his own included.

Treating all situations as though they might be Karmic in nature, an Oriental attempts to approach everything which happens to him with love, patience, and understanding.

Through belief in reincarnation and astrology in the Orient, even ecology is affected. I never saw litter in Japan, nor deliberate misuse of nature (except in those areas influenced by Western ideals and materialism). The most poverty-stricken Japanese people, living in the slums, are clean, as are the humble shacks in which they live.

I discovered the reason for this. When a Japanese believes in reincarnation, he desires to keep the land as he himself would like to see it when and if he comes back to the same place in a later life. Everyone in Japan loves nature, and even in the smallest yard you will find a garden and people who attend it. The hope of a Japanese is to return to the beauty he has left in his present life.

Through belief in astrology, certain Karmic aspects of personality are brought to light, making it easier for the individual to live out this Karma.

Both the teachings of reincarnation and astrology bring one into more awareness of himself and of those with whom he comes in contact.

There are several teachings in the West that most of us seem to abide by. They are not only wrong, they are also destructive and evil. What can one expect from a civilization that teaches:

"Live every day as if it were the last!"

"You only live once!"

"Grab every bit of material happiness while you can!"

"There's no tomorrow!"

These adages tend to make the Westerner selfish, materialistic, and decadent. They teach us to do whatever we please, whenever we please, even at the expense of those around us.

In the East, the adages are completely opposite from ours. And I do believe that if we are to survive, we must adopt many of the teachings of the East.

We should each strive to change our materialistic viewpoints to:

"Live every day as if it were the first!"

"You *do* live more than once!"

"Accept every bit of spirituality offered you while you can!"

"There is tomorrow . . . and tomorrow . . . and tomorrow!"

Index